Ron McCreight is the longest serving "plugger" in the history of the music business, starting in a Tin Pan Alley music publishing house during the 1960s and working through the next 7 decades adopting various roles. His joint venture Promotion/PR company, with Pete Waterman, *Sharp End,* went on to become the most successful of its kind, representing over 200 top 40 hit singles in its 15-year history. In the 70s McCreight combined his promotion and publishing activities with writing a weekly column for US trade magazine, Record World, when he interviewed some of the world's top stars. More recently, he has operated independently for various record companies and publishers including Eagle Rock and Cherry Red.

This work is dedicated to my friends, family and colleagues with whom I have had the privilege of living and working alongside over these many years:

Annette Barrett – my darling wife who saved and made my life!

Robert Lemon – for his companionship during some very tough times but always making sure we had some fun.

David Mindel – a true friend whose talent and determination was my motivation in the early days and has been ever since.

Eddie O'loughlin – my American 'brother' whose inspiration has been my guiding light.

Ken Slidders – best friend from the age of seven whose support and bass playing brought me through my early days in Tin Pan Alley.

David Howells – for his confidence and belief in me from the very beginning.

Pete Waterman – for giving me the biggest break of my career.

Ian Rowe – a very special man unlike anyone else I've known in the record business and a sheer delight to work with.

Colin Peter – for being his first choice plugger for more than twenty years.

Phil Swern – whose vast knowledge has been essential but his friendship even more so.

Dave Clarke – for his energy and enthusiasm which picked me up to see me through the 'second half'.

Adrian Williams – lessons in how to be the perfect plugger, never a dull moment.

Mauro Dirago – a pure gem in so many different ways with unshakable optimism.

Alex Lester – his support so often saved the day and giving me the opportunity to be a minor broadcaster myself.

Graham Robertson – a brilliant researcher and another enthusiast whose energy was infectious. His trust in me was extremely flattering.

Ron McCreight

In at the Sharp End (Stories from the Front Line of the Music Business)

AUSTIN MACAULEY PUBLISHERS™

LONDON • CAMBRIDGE • NEW YORK • SHARJAH

A CIP catalogue record for this title is available from the British Library.

ISBN 9781398464780 (Paperback)
ISBN 9781398464797 (ePub e-book)

www.austinmacauley.com

First Published 2022
Austin Macauley Publishers Ltd®
1 Canada Square
Canary Wharf
London
E14 5AA

Thanks go to: Lee Martin of Getty Images, Mark Hagen and David Stark for many of these photographs.
Pier Pagano, Sarah Wooldridge & Bob Massie (IMG) for their wisdom and guidance in the literary world.
Weidenfeld & Nicolson publishers
St Martins Griffin publishers

My love and gratitude to all the wonderful, talented singers, musicians, songwriters and producers, without whom we would have nothing (but silence).

Table of Contents

Foreword

I think everyone can make a guess at how the music industry works. Or how they think it works. The reality is rather different and at times frankly bonkers.

One man has devoted his working life to making musical artists successful. That man is Ron McCreight. The hardest working, longest serving and successful of the 'pluggers'. The fact he has survived so long in a cutthroat industry is the testament to his talent and tenacity. The fact he has emerged with his sanity intact is frankly a miracle!

In At The Sharp End is one man's journey from his start as a junior in Music Publishing through to record promotion working with some of the world's premier artists, songwriters and producers. Over the years Ron has worked with the best (and some of the worst depending upon your musical taste).

Writing as someone who has played thousands of songs on the radio over the last 40 years including hundreds of new releases, I've been "plugged" by Ron many times. One thing has always come through which sets Ron apart. Integrity! Not a word you associate with promotions, necessarily.

Ron always knew the music I'd like to present to you my radio shows. So he'd turn up with the records/CDs/downloads (as the formats changed) and often but not always he was right.

If you like music, you'll like Ron. He really likes music.

At heart he is still the Mod in the sharp suit queuing to see The Small Faces. I suspect he'd have done it all for nothing.

This is his story and it is as fascinating as it's revealing.

Introduction

From the cultural revolution of the 1960s, through every decade since, music has been at the core of every young person's life – I have been lucky enough to have been there through each of these decades operating in many different areas of the record and music publishing business! It has been an amazing roller coaster ride of huge success, some failure but always working with some of the world's most special talents. There is an abundance of books written about theh music industry but never before covering such a wide range of genre and in such intimate terms, coming from the perspective of promoting artists, record plugging, music publishing and journalism.

My journey has taken me from Denmark Street (Tin Pan Alley), the UK centre of music in the sixties; Record World (USA) magazine columnist in the seventies ; the launch of Radio 1 ; the launch of Capital Radio ; independent music publishing ; the Stock, Aitken, Waterman phenomenon of the eighties – forming Sharp End Promotions with Robert Lemon which became the most successful independent promotion company in the history of the business ; Cherry Red Records, who are the longest surviving indie label in the UK ; Eagle Rock/Vision, pioneers of music DVD ; and now as a sole operating plugger serving the UK record business. A fulfilling and rewarding career covering fifty eight years and counting. And…there is so much more.

I'd like to think that anyone interested in popular music will enjoy reading this study of a fascinating industry and stories such as how Kylie came so close to missing her big chance ; how Simon Cowell lost it all ; when George Martin met the Beatles ; what motivated Bob Geldof to stage the greatest live concert in history ; Take That's initial failure to get a record deal ; why Boyzone's record company refused to release their first single ; and the rise (and subsequent disappearance) of the richest man in music ever, Clive Calder, largely thanks to Britney, Billy.

Artists and Songwriters featured include (in alphabetical order):

Allan Clarke (The Hollies)

Bob Geldof

Blow Monkeys

Boyzone

Brother Beyond

Burt Bacharach

Christopher Cross

Danni Minogue

David Frost

Dodgy

Elkie Brooks

Gary Benson

Gary Brooker (Procol Harum)

Gene Pitney

George Martin

Graham Gouldman (10 CC)

Hazell Dean

Holly Johnson

Ian McLagan (Small Faces/Faces)

Jack Bruce

Jason Donovan

Justin Hayward (The Moody Blues)

Kylie Minogue

Leo Sayer

Marc Almond

Mick Brown

Mike McCartney (The Scaffold)

Neil Sedaka

Pat Sharp

Paul Jones

Pete Waterman

Petula Clark

Ray Davies (The Kinks)

Roger Hodgson (Supertramp)

Ronnie Wood (The Rolling Stones)

Samantha Fox

Shakin' Stevens

Simon Cowell

Sinitta

Sonia

Suzi Quatro

Take That

The Fall

Tom Jones

This Is My Story

I am sitting at my computer to write this book on the February 19, 2014, nearly 50 years since I started as a song plugger for Tin Pan Alley based music publishing company, Noel Gay Music! The day goes very well but is not necessarily typical by any means!

Now that Radio 2 is the biggest national UK radio stations, it has become a weekly routine to have my current single considered at their playlist meeting held at high noon every Wednesday in their central London HQ, Wogan House in Great Portland Street.

This week I am pitching relatively unknown Irish band Picturehouse and their single, *Rules Of Science*, a great record but no matter how good, it is always a long shot unless you are already a well-established name. So, I do the final round of lobbying around the building and then cross my fingers. Next I head for a meeting with another new artist, Alex Hart and her manager/producer, Neil Stainton and head of her record company, Right Track, Colin Peter. All goes well and we hatch a promotion plan for the coming months.

Now for the real highlight of the day, a trip to Jools Holland's studio in Greenwich to attend and oversee Marc Almond's participation in the radio show being recorded for future broadcast on Radio 2. The Helicon Mountain studio is a very special place, steeped in music and modelled on the iconic 'Prisoner' TV series from the '60s (a Jools fascination). His band is brilliant and Marc performs his live song, a Dinah Washington classic, *Stranger On Earth*, perfectly. An in-depth interview follows, so good that the session over runs but everyone is happy including Jools, producers Mark Hagen and Janine Maya-Smith and vitally, Marc himself.

Marc Almond performing with the Jools Holland Band for Radio 2,
February 19, 2014

Then, finally the wait is over and the new Radio 2 playlist is announced –
the Picturehouse single IS added and the good news travels fast to Ireland and
back to everyone involved – it is a fantastic result given the competition. This
completes a very special day and reminds me why I am still doing this job after
so any years!

Chapter 1
Tin Pan Alley

Denmark Street 1963

Rolling back the years to August 19, 1963, when I walked through the door of The Noel Gay Organisation, 24 Denmark Street, London WC2, to start my first job, eight days before my sixteenth birthday, little did I know that this was the start of such a most fascinating life – dealing with the weird and wonderful; the talented, the losers, the good guys and the time wasters.

Although I was just a number cruncher in the accounts department, I was soon to be surrounded by some of the greatest musicians of the time – it was The Swingin' Sixties, a wonderful time to be in London working for a music company!

At lunchtime I would walk down Denmark Street staring at the sheet music on display in all the windows and the awesome display of guitars in Macaris music store. The impact of seeing The Rolling Stones wandering out of Regent Sounds Studios was immense – they were recording their first ever album for Decca Records; David Bowie was hanging out in the Giaconda cafe; Peter Noone (Herman's Hermits) was feeding a parking metre. I was certainly in the right place but I had to find a way of getting noticed and moving out of the accounts department and into the creative division.

After nearly three years, finally my big break came and it was just before the launch of Radio 1 which promised to offer up many more opportunities in music air play. Although I was slightly on boss Richard Armitage's radar through my band being booked by the agency division, it was hard to gain his attention. Then one day he was marching through the accounts department asking if anyone knew of American star, Del Shannon – I spoke up quoting his hits *Hat's Off To Larry*, *Swiss Maid* and *Runaway*.

He quickly put two and two together – a guitarist and music enthusiast – "What are you doing in accounts, you should be in the music publishing department."

I was immediately offered a job as a song plugger and although I had no idea what that entailed and my parents insisted that my accounts job was kept open to see how it went with the plugging, there was no going back. They need not have worried, a trial period stretched into a lifetime.

One of my first assignments was to take a Russ Conway single, *The Crunch* to the BBC Light Programme studios located in Aeolian Hall, New Bond Street in an attempt to get it played. I was right in at the deep end and many problems arose. Firstly, I was not exactly a Russ Conway fan (a cheesy, gimmick ridden jangle piano player); airplay opportunities were severely restricted in those days as the Musicians Union insisted that a large percentage of music on the BBC was live; but the main issue was that an unknown young guy with long hair was attempting to tel' them what to play. A fast learner, I smartened up realising that if the security guards thought you looked respectable, you had free entry into the premises and to be taken seriously by the men in suits who were the producers, you had to wear one. Generally, things were about to improve dramatically with the launch of Radio 1 set up to pacify the young audience after the closure of the pirate radio stations, taking many of the DJs with them including my friend Duncan Johnson. For the first time the UK had a national station with a full on music policy in stark contrast to the previous Light Programme and Home Service!

The official Radio 1 launch photo in September 1967. Those pictured include my friend Duncan Johnson (back row fourth left), Terry Wogan, John Peel, Dave Cash, Jimmy Young. Only Tony Blackburn is still broadcasting.

However, in those early days the limited 'needle time' imposed by the MU still provided a challenge so bands were required to record bespoke sessions in a BBC studio attempting to sound exactly like the original record which may have taken days, weeks or months to perfect. They even had to pass a BBC audition before being booked – this included The Beatles, The Stones, The Who, The Small Faces etc. Running alongside Radio 1, to serve an older audience was Radio 2 who had even less needle time so the studios in Maida Vale and Aeolian Hall were continuously frill of big bands, orchestras and trios including many of those represented by Noel Gay. I distinctly remember visiting these sessions – a regular performer was Mexican pianist, Pepe Jaramillo who remarkable had 20 albums available on EMI. One of my duties was to act as paymaster to his musicians as part of a rather convoluted system, the company would invoice the BBC for Pepe's fee as well as the musicians. I would then take their money in cash to the studios which of course made me very popular. Other regulars were the Geoff Love Orchestra, and the aforementioned Russ Conway who once demanded I sat with him at his piano to turn over the music and although at the time I had no idea, he was Gay… I was learning fast!

The most exciting live music derived from BBC lunchtime shows including three a week from The Playhouse Theatre in London's Northumberland Avenue. As part of my early networking opportunities, I was given tickets and £5 in petty cash to buy the producers drinks after the show in the nearby Sherlock Holmes pub. To start the week was 'Monday Monday' with the resident big band being the Ray McVay orchestra. Bizarrely they would 'cover' current hits alongside the real deal from all the great bands of the day – the Rolling Stones, The Who, The Small Faces and the UK debut performance of the Bee Gees who only had one song at the time, *Massachusetts*.

Wednesday was 'Parade Of The Pops' hosted by Bob Miller and The Millermen which enjoyed a similar format and the finishing of the week with the Joe Loss Show. I loved every minute of these shows but I found the after show pub experience rather daunting, not to mention being able to handle lunchtime drinking albeit half of bitter (the producers may have indulged a little more though). Joe Loss personally provided the sandwiches on Fridays whereas us pluggers had to fund all the rest, in this period there was also a Tuesday show called 'Pop In' but there was no live music involved, just interviews conducted by host Keith Fordyce who I remembered from introducing The Beatles at the NME Pollwinners Wembley concerts. Another of my somewhat dubious duties at that time was to plug brass and military bands – the basement in our Denmark Street base was full of scores and parts of an innumerable number of our copyrights and I was appointed to get them used as much as possible. As most of the brass bands were based in the north of England, the exercise involved spending hours on the phone trying to reach and then convince the respective band leaders of the merit of our catalogue.

One of these, the Brighouse and Rastrick band from Yorkshire actually had a hit single with their 'Woganised' version of *Floral Dance*. Another Yorkshire based outfit, The Black Dyke Mills band bizarrely were signed by Paul McCartney to his Apple label, and scored with their version of *Yellow Submarine*! Military bands were a completely different ballgame – the process here meant visiting various military bases to meet the directors of music. One remarkable encounter was with Colonel Cecil Jaeger (known as Jiggs) who led the Brigade of Guards. Quite a character as it transpired – on entering his office he immediately brought out a bottle of whiskey and after a brief conversation promised to include one of my arrangements in his repertoire. Leaving very happy, if slightly wobbly I had to cross the parade ground and you can only imagine the comments from the troops observing me in my sharp mod suit and long hair!

Although I was still in the accounts department when our duo, Peter and Gordon released their first single, Lennon-McCartney's *World Without Love* it meant the company, in my eyes was slowly moving into a more credible direction and with the record reaching No 1 throughout the world, including the USA, we could attract artists that were more attractive to me. First up was Paul Jones who left the super cool Manfred Mann band to go solo with a record deal from EMI which coincided with my start in the music department. I recall paying in his advance cheque to the company's local bank – a staggering amount of money, just eye-watering. This was rapidly followed with the signing of The Scaffold whose front man was Paul McCartney's younger brother Mike (McGear)! I loved all these Beatle connections as at the time they were simply the biggest thing on the planet. Peter (Asher) is Jane's brother – Paul's girlfriend of the moment so no coincidence they pulled in those songs including the follow up, *Nobody I Know* (although that only just made the Top 10). The guys went on to have a string of hits and sold out NYC's Shea Stadium shortly after The Beatles world breaking concert there in 1965.

Meanwhile, Paul Jones was off to a flying start with *High Time* reaching No 4 in the UK singles chart and the follow up, *I've Been A Bad, Bad Boy* finishing one short at No 5. I had the most awesome assignment of accompanying Paul to one of his 'Top of the Pops' appearances in the BBC studios in Lime Grove, Shepherds Bush (before moving to White City). This was actually my second experience of such fan hysteria! Outside the studio, Paul's Rolls Royce was surrounded by thousands of screaming girls and with so little security in those days, it was almost life threatening but a real buzz nonetheless.

My first experience of such highly charged outbursts of emotion, was actually surrounding the Beatles…! I was lucky enough to obtain an audience ticket for ITV's highly prestigious, long running 'Sunday Night at the London Palladium' in 1963. This was the official start of Beatlemania, such hysteria had never been seen before and the producers knew how to wind up an audience – it kicked off right at the start of the show, as, replacing the usual dance troupe opening, the curtain rose to see the fab four performing *Please Please Me* – it was just insane. Several minutes later, calm was resumed so the show could continue with the band eventually performing four more songs to close the show. I then joined the mass crowds in the rush around to the stage door in Great Marlborough street in a vain attempt to see the fab four.

Other personal highlights with Paul were: attending his Leicester Square film premier, 'Privilege' which also starred sixties icon, Jean Shrimpton; and sitting in on some of his vocal sessions, my first of many visits to the historic EMI Studios in Abbey Road.

It was truly a shock that Paul's pop career stalled after only two years! A misguided choice for the third single, Thinkin' Aint For Me, proved fatal.

However, he eventually found his true identity in the blues and developed a highly successful career on the live music circuit before becoming a presenter of Radio 2's Blues Show which ran for an incredible 32 years until April 2018. He continues performing to this day with his own The Blues Band and The Manfreds' which features various former members including Mike D'Abo (who replaced him in the original 60s' line up), Tom McGuiness and Mike Hugg who were also founder members.

Throughout this time my boss, Richard Armitage was determined to keep me grounded and expected me continue with dealing with the company's sheet music sales but when The Scaffold had their first hit with Thank U Very Much, I found renewed motivation when thousands of orders flooded in although it was extremely hard work to keep up with the demand. There was also some professional satisfaction to be gained in that I had designed the edition too. Until this point I had kept things ticking over with old stock of titles such as La Vie En Rose, My Heart Belongs To You, Run Rabbit Run and You've Done Something To My Heart! Things really exploded a year later when McGear, McGough and Gorman struck gold with their Christmas No 1 Lily The Pink. The record sold over a million and the sheet music several thousand which was arguably an even higher achievement!

By the end of the 1960s, I had built my confidence and was flattered that everyone involved wanted my view on whether Lily The Pink or McGough's poem based, Buttons Of Your Mind should be the A SIDE of the release. This joyously involved my second visit to the Abbey Road Studios where I quickly insisted that Lily should lead the way and although Radio 1 airplay was extremely difficult to obtain, the high rating Saturday Club producer, Bill Bebb gave me his support which proved to be the real breakthrough.

Doing the promotional rounds with The Scaffold was just amazing fun – three very different personalities; with Mike wanting to be the serious pop star, Roger a serious and accomplished poet and John Gorman a natural comedian who went on to co-host with Chris Tarrant, ITV's Saturday morning show, 'Tiswas'. One particular interview for Radio 1 finished in chaos with everyone, me included, on the floor laughing, sheer hysterics after something John had said.

There were also several visits to 'Top of the Pops', the first one still at the Lime Grove studios before moving to TV Centre in 1969. The guys were also very happy for me to hang out with them at EMI studios and one memorable night, 'our kid', Paul McCartney showed up to help salvage the (eventually failed) single, Stop Blowing Those Charity Bubbles with the session ending in all of us around the microphone doing hand claps. Somehow I ended up buying the drinks at the nearby pub at the end of the night.

I met up with Mike again in 2016, some 39 years later, to promote the reissued 'McGough and McGear' album for Cherry Red Records (originally

E.M.I. Studios, now Abbey Road

released by EMI in 1968). It was as if it was only yesterday, nothing had changed except the colour of our hair.

In 1967 such was the drawing power of anything Beatle related, guests rolling up to play on the album included Jimi Hendrix, Brian Auger, Spencer Davis and Graham Nash (who also sang on 'Lily The Pink')! A fabulous experience for me as all these guys were my heroes – all this and I was still only 20 years old.

With Mike (McGear) McCartney at The Under The Bridge venue,
Chelsea For Cherry Red's 40th anniversary party

If anything Mike had become more open and interesting after all these years – it must have been difficult being the brother of a mega star – now he was happy to talk freely about Paul and how he changed his name in the '60s from McCartney to McGear in order to avoid being accused on cashing in. In choosing this pseudonym, he explained it was between fab and gear, the hip words in Merseyside of the time. One of the most interesting interviews for the 2016 campaign with Mike was for Johnnie Walker's Radio 2 show, 'Sounds of the '70s' but by way of contrast I brought in Roger McGough to guest on Jools Holland's show. Another delightful reunion, Roger is such a warm, friendly man and an amazing poet whose career has taken a more serious direction with regular spot on BBC Radio 4 as well as many voice overs including a long running Waitrose campaign.

With Roger McGough at Jools Holland's Helicon Studio in Greenwich

Before George Martin unearthed the most successful band on the planet, he had produced all kinds of records including Bernard Cribbins' *Right Said Fred* and *A Hole In The Ground* both songs we published at Noel Gay. We also published his composition *By George* especially commissioned as a new David Frost TV theme. So along with the entire NEMS stable of artists such as Cilla Black, Gerry and the Pacemakers and Billy J Kramer – all having No 1 singles, somehow he also found time to produce the first Scaffold single, *2 Day's Monday* (seemingly as a favour to Paul) which failed to chart. During this time, I only briefly met George but much later, in 2012, I did have the opportunity to get to know him while promoting his 'Produced by George Martin' DVD for Eagle Vision. Although his manager was cautious about George running on the promotion trail at the age of 86, he did agree to an interview on Radio 2's Steve Wright show which I set up easily. It went so well that I gently enquired about doing some more – he politely agreed but not until he had his three-week holiday. So, exactly three weeks later, I brought him in to do the Robert Elms Show for BBC Radio London which my producer friend, Graham Robertson booked in an instant. However, a few days prior to the set date, Graham casually mentioned that Robert was definitely NOT a Beatles fan. I had a sleepless night wondering how this would go but I need not have worried as Robert loves Matt Monroe and George has produced all his albums. As we left the studio George commented on how much he had enjoyed the interview as it was so refreshing not to be asked about The Beatles! In the final interview with Shaun Keaveny for BBC 6 Music, George was asked about the Abbey Road sessions – he answered with the story of the instrumental solo on *In My Life*:

"We would often leave space for an instrumental solo on a track, usually a guitar solo from George (Harrison) but when we recorded *In My Life*, the boys took a pub break so I played around on the piano. I was inept so had to slow down the tape to play the solo – when sped up it sounded like a Harpsichord."

Steve Wright enquired as to George's current and future activates. – "When you get to my age you spend an awful amount of time having medical appointments," was his down to earth answer.

The signing of The Beatles was touched on but was best described in George's book, 'All You Need is Ears': 'It was in April 1962 that I got the phone call from Syd Coleman, a friend and one of the music industry's nice guys, who was head of Ardmore and Beechwood (EMI's publishing company) with offices above the iconic HMV shop in London's Oxford Street. He said, "I don't know if you'd be interested but there's a chap who's come in with a tape of a group he runs. They haven't got a recording contract and I wonder if you would like to see him and listen to what he's go?"

"Certainly," I said, "I'm willing to listen to anything. Ask him to come and see me."

"OK, I will – his name is Brian Epstein!"

Sir George Martin at Abbey
Road Studio 2 In the 1960s' Beatle days.

Abbey Road Studio 2 when I visited
with David McAlmont who performed
live for Radio 2's Jo Whiley Show on
April 7, 2011

The recording, to put it kindly, was by no means a knock-out. I could well understand that people had turned it down. I suggested to Brain that he should bring the boys to Abbey Road studios for a recording test. Unknown to me at the time, he groaned inwardly. It seemed to him that he had heard that sort of thing before, but we went ahead and fixed a date for June 6. It was love at first sight… It is now common knowledge that this meeting was Epstein's final chance of a Record deal for The Beatles, having been rejected by every record company including Decca and even by another division of EMI.

Years of extraordinary success followed but George, somewhat dissatisfied with his own deal with EMI, formed his own Associated Independent Recording (AIR) with other former staffers, John Burgess (who I knew from his work with Peter and Gordon) and Ron Richards, The Hollies producer. Initially a production company, they went on to build a state-of-the-art studio based near London's Oxford Circus which still exists albeit now in Hampstead, north London. Another hi-tech complex was set up on the Caribbean island of Montserrat where several classic albums were recorded before a hurricane forced its closure in 1989.

It is testament to George's highly impressive all-round ability that he could direct operations on a technical level being qualified in all things to do with sound – frequencies/hertz measurements etc, as well as being a virtuoso musician, arrange, conduction and composer. In his 1979 book he even predicted the coming of the digital age, around 20 years ahead of its time.

It was such a sad day – March 9, 2016, when George passed away, shortly after his 90th birthday. I was honoured to be asked to make a tribute live on his local station BBC Radio Oxford.

'All You Need Is Ears' – St Martin's Griffin, published 1979.

Moving into the 1970s, my career was really moving forward as I signed my first songwriter, Gary Benson – a significant step taking me into more pastures unknown.

This was the beginning of the classic singer-songwriter era and, a little naively, I considered that Gary was among the very best along with Elton John, Cat Stevens, Neil Diamond and James Taylor.

Rather strangely a publishing colleague, Ian Ralfini at Robbins Music introduced me to Gary suggesting I would do a better job for him – maybe there was some kind of personality clash as this was so unusual. Gary had just released his first single, *Kentucky* on EMI's Columbia label and Ian was happy for me to assign the copyright to Noel Gay and then take over his career. The single failed to chart so he was immediately dropped by EMI and my first task was to secure a new deal. We recorded a few very low budget demos at Regent Sounds Studios and I shopped them around before I found a taker in Larry Page who had just started a new label, Penny Farthing having terminated his partnership with Beatles publisher, Dick James in Page One Records (with success from The Troggs and Vanity Fair). Larry shared my enthusiasm and provided a good budget for an album to be produced by my flat mate, David Paramor and arranged by Christopher Gunning who has since become one of the UKs most accomplished classical composer/arranger.

I was asked to write the sleeve notes:

"Many words will be written and spoken in years to come about Gary Benson whose vocal and composing talents are superbly demonstrated on this – his first album. I will start the ball rolling by saying that his collection of Gary's songs are only twelve out of many written over the past two years, all of which are of equal quality and there is no doubt you will be hearing those too before long, as well as the many yet to come. I will not attempt to describe in detail the songs on this album, as you will certainly appreciate the beauty of melody and depth of lyrics which typify Gary's natural ability on first hearing. So, now listen and see how the songs speak for themselves."

Well, I'm not sure how many words have been written and spoken about Gary since 1970 but he certainly had a few record deals over the following 10 years, never to be repeated without having some big hit singles.

Next up was Miki Dallon's Birth Records, a subsidiary of Young Blood who had enjoyed several hits with Mac and Katie Kissoon, Don Fardon as well as Rod Stewart under the pseudonym of Python Lee Jackson. My friend Dave Williams who I had met on the plugging circuit had turned record producer and knew Miki so helped with the pitch. He loved the demos so we had a deal although I don't remember it being that simple. Gary's 'The Concert' album was the label's first release and the single, *Sausalito* was plugged to death at Radio 1 but in the end we had another failure.

By this time, I had been joined by my long term friend, David Mindel to generally assist me in the music division and without question this was the highlight of my time with the company. David was one half of duo, David and David being produced by Elton John's man, Gus Dudgeon for EMI. They were signed to the agency department but no gigs were forthcoming and the record failed. So I approached David to join me in some plugging while he could keep on writing songs. It transpired that he had a talent for finding good restaurants which was becoming extremely important in wining and dining radio producers. Otherwise plugging was not really for him so we spent more and more time recording demos, mainly in the nearby Orange Studios (owned by John Miles, famous for the classic 'Music' manager, Cliff Cooper). We were joined by his 'agent', Andrew Peter on drums (he had played in A Band Of Angels with John Gaydon and David Wilkinson who with manager, David Enthoven had joined Noel Gay as agents plus Mike D'Abo on vocals) and Gary Benson helped out on guitar (I played very poor piano). It was a natural development that David and Gary should write together and we demoed their song *Don't Throw It All Away* entering it into the Song For Europe contest with The Shadows performing the six contenders, we came last. However, much of the music business recognised that this was a hit song and B and C Records stepped up wanting it to be their first release on their new Mooncrest imprint. They really had huge belief in the song as the first recording really didn't work so they started again with Rob Young stepping in with a beautiful arrangement so we were finally set to go (after massive recording costs hurting them badly, ultimately fatally).

I set about plugging the single at Radio 1 and they willingly gave their support in the build up to the release. During the campaign I regularly visited the nearby Nellie Dean pub with B and C's in-house plugger, Brian Haynes to compare notes. On one of these visits he broke the news that the company was going into liquidation so I immediately retrieved the tapes; set about negotiating with the creditors; found yet another record label in State Records – all accomplished with haste, during an oppressive heatwave – time was of the essence in order to maintain the momentum building on Radio 1. State was affiliated to the major, Polydor and set up by two of their former senior executives, John Fruin and Wayne Bickerton. They knew I had a hot record so gambled on manufacturing sufficient stock to deliver a hit – a real drama but in the end a fantastic result selling over 100,000 copies with Gary performing the song on 'Top of the Pops' twice.

Gary Benson's "Don't Throw
It All Away" first edition on B
and C Records Moon Crest Label

The version finally released by Polydor's
State Records in July 1975

The Polydor connection offered up a support slot on a European tour by The Hollies including a date at London's Royal Albert Hall. However, there was a substantial cost facture including a 'buy-on' fee, musician's fees, transport and accommodation. The small budget was disappearing fast with the addition of some large bar bills – rock and roll I guess. The end result was that I had to drive the van around the German leg of the tour but all things considered it was huge fun and a wonderful experience. Gary was never really comfortable being on the road and complained constantly that he had given up his job as a cigar salesman for THIS?

However, it led to Gary co-writing songs with Hollies front man, Allan Clarke for his solo album, 'Legendary Heroes' released by Polydor in the UK and the iconic Atlantic label in the USA. This was a golden era for Gary as, thanks to more of our demos being pitched around, he had cuts with Cilla Black, Georgie Fame, and biggest hit of all, John Travolta's debut, *Let Her In*, a No 1 record in America. There was initially a problem as when Gary heard the Travolta recording he said "he's destroyed my song, you have to stop it being released."

I did nothing and thankfully a few days later a telex arrived to say the single had charted in the US at No 55 with a bullet. When Gary heard the news he was quick to ask if I had taken any action. The year before The Shadows Eurovision adventure, Gary had come close with another Dave Mindel co-write, *Someday* which made the final six(but finishing last) in another 'Song For Europe' contest, this time fronted by Oliva Newton-John. Unsuccessful in Europe but her recording was included in a multimillion selling album.

During the process of plugging Gary's songs; legendary record man, Clive Davies was alerted and summoned us to go to New York to play him some more songs. He was interested but wanted to hear more so we then visited his suite at London's Dorchester Hotel – he heard three more songs which seemed to do the trick. Clive offered up a deal to record an album with his Arista label to be produced in Los Angeles by local producer, Spencer Proffer. The budget provided for Gary to take up residency at Hollywood's Sunset Marquee hotel but with the sessions running too slow for his liking, he called me every day to complain that all he was doing was lying by the swimming pool – the never satisfied, Gary Benson.

When the album was finally finished, Arista released a single in the USA and I made regular trips to their offices in New York to monitor and encourage promotional efforts. However, when the record failed to chart, Clive Davies lost interest and there was a rumour it was all about holding Gary's songs for his pet artist, Barry Manilow.

It was left to UK CEO, Charles Levison to break the bad news that the deal was terminated but we could own the rights in order to place it with another label. Another friend, Aaron Sixx who was also close to the album's producers Matthew Macauley and Fred Molin , stepped up with an offer to release it in the UK on his newly launched, Aura Records but he could not stretch to paying an advance. The priority was to get it on to the market so we went ahead with the deal and 'Moonlight Walking' was given a release date for March 1980. As things transpired, after more than 10 years of hard graft, it was the end of my relationship with Gary! Unknown to me he had entered a song into the 'Song for Europe' (Eurovision) contest and had again successfully made the short list.

In those days, record companies competed to pick up these records as the TV exposure was huge and Warner Bros came in for Gary's track. However, this put Gary in breach of his Aura agreement and I was subpoenaed to attend a court hearing as a witness – he had denied all knowledge of the Aura deal! There was no winner – his Eurovision song failed and by then Charles Levison had become head of Warner so instantly dropped Gary for the second time. The single was never released but it left Aura in the clear to release their album. Karma had played its part and there was no going back for our relationship.

Throughout this time, mainly driven by David Mindel, we kept the demo machine running bringing in musicians who would work for a pint and a snack in the White Lion pub, along with the sheer fun of it all. This included my best friend, Ken Slidders who played bass in my own band and Bill Pitt who had replaced me in the Noel Gay accounts department.

David brought in some fresh faces from a consortium he had formed called Saturday (their only day off from their day jobs) including Mike Read who later became a Radio 1 DJ. The most successful song to emerge, *If (Would It Turn Out Wrong)* by Esprit de Corps, was picked up by Dick James' JAM label, run by his son Stephen. David turned this into quite a lush production and started to sound like a hit when Radio 1 made it their breakfast show, Tony Blackburn's record of the week.

Then came the unbelievable news that the golden ticket of TV, 'Top of the Pops' offered up their new release slot. By this time Mike Read was uncontactable so the band had no choice but to continue without him, only for Mike to turn up unexpectedlyat TV centre threatening to take legal action – after heated exchanges, he was ejected.

Meanwhile the airplay continued and a press campaign backed up all our efforts. Then came the bombshell – the BBC were alerted to the fact that two pluggers (David and myself) were behind the project so Radio 1 dropped the track overnight – it finally disappeared without trace.

In spite of this disappointment we continued to finish what were essentially demos into full blown productions and place them as singles to various record labels. We came up with some rather bizarre band names (Dog Rose, Bollard, Hobbit, Happy Ending, Shovel etc.) and they all featured either Gary Benson, David or me on lead vocals! The exception came from Maltese crooner, Jon

Lukas who was introduced to me by budding entrepreneur, Henry Hadaway. Jon recorded Gary Benson's *I Can't Afford To Lose* and I managed to get a deal with EMI who released the single on their Columbia label, I was credited as being co-producer. Henry pledged a healthy marketing budget being extremely keen to do whatever might be necessary to get the single into the UK charts. The only idea we had was to stage a lunch party for which we chose the swanky Mayfair restaurant, Quaglinos. This was the perfect way to spend a large amount of Henry's money, or so we thought. A large orchestra was hired along with TV producer, Royston Mayo to stage the event – he in turn brought in a (rather too tall) model to introduce the artist – Jon is only just over five feet tall. Interestingly Royston did not attend the actually event. So, following a rather embarrassing introduction, Jon's nerves got the better of him and he missed several cues turning his performance into a complete shamble. Such humiliation witnessed by the mass media from radio, television and the press: Henry's reaction – "Was he good?"; My boss, Armitage – silence.

Key Radio 1 producer, Ron Belchier, not known for his friendly, easy going nature – "Where does Mr Lukas come from?"

"Malta," I replied.

Mr Belchier: "Why doesn't he just go back there then?"

I just wanted to put the whole thing down to experience but it was not that simple as the following morning I was to make my first visit to New York City with Armitage and David Frost – sitting together on a plane for seven straight hours. You could say he made me suffer in silence but eventually he just told me… never again, then moved on.

In the meantime, to add insult to injury, Mr Hadaway failed to pay the bills and as I had booked everything, I was held responsible. Eventually he gave me some cash to fund some more studio time which I used to clear the debts and secured the studios by way of a favour. This session resulted in Henry's own Satril Records first releases, *I Need Your Love* by Bollard which was in fact sung by David's friend, the very accomplished David Ballantyne (Henry's first choice failed to show up) and written by another Noel Gay contract writer, Hugh Pattison. Although Satril was a good outlet for our material for a while, I slowly but surely started to extract myself from any further involvement as my instincts told me this was not the way forward.

By this time David had established an impressive pool of brilliant musicians with good access to major studios and engineers, so justifiably, he pushed for his own production company within Noel Gay and was subsequently relieved of his plugging duties being replaced by another 'solid gold' man in David (Ions) who had been working with Tony Hatch's – Mr and Mrs music company. Everything ran rather well for around a year with further releases coming from major labels, Decca, EMI and Polydor all paying reasonable advances. But, unfortunately no hits emerged so Armitage instructed me to close down the production company meaning we had to let David go! I begged Armitage to give him back his old job but this was in vein although I think David had already decided to move on to something completely new.

As the true gentlemen he is, David handled the news really well and we are close friends to this day. In fact, he had already decided to move into the world of TV commercials with his former singing partner David Seys who was well connected with all the ad agencies – Mingles Music was launched in 1975. As an extremely generous gesture I was invited to play acoustic guitar on his first assignment for Cadburys although there were many more talented musicians who could have done the job.

I was so happy to see his company flourishing and becoming the leading jingle company of the time receiving countless commissions from many major brand including Maxwell House Rothmans, Kellogg's, Bisto etc. David also wrote several TV themes including the long running *Jim'll Fix It*; David also received an Ivor Novello award nomination.

I did find working without David difficult but the new David (Ions) was a real gem and we formed a new publishing company with his former boss Tony Hatch and his brother in law, Les Burgess – all very exciting and great fun, but my biggest break came in 1976 when John Travolta recorded Gary Benson's *Let Her In*, the result of a meeting at the MIDEM music festival in Cannes (more on that later).

I had met producer and label owner, Bob Reno through my friend Eddie O'Loughlin. Bob offered a deal on the song along the lines of him getting the sub-publishing rights for North America if it was released within six months. A massive hit in the USA as was the follow up, happily a David Mindel co-write, *Whenever I'm Away From You*.

However, in his usual rather dismissive way, Armitage offered me a small bonus (the song earned thousands of pounds) and immediately sought to steer me away into projects he considered were more important. Not all bad as I was privileged to work alongside some serious celebrities including David Frost, who was the hottest thing on TV in the late sixties, through the seventies. He presented three shows a week in the USA as well as his high rating 'The Frost Programme' in the UK which followed the BBC's 'Frost Report'.

Mr Frost had abundant energy which was very evident when travelling with him on what was then BOAC (now BA) to New York and staying in his suite at the five star Essex House Hotel on Central Park South. His lifestyle was just insane and the only way to get his attention was to have early breakfast meetings as he came off a plane – this involved some serious eating as well as business, with steak, eggs, hash browns, etc., the works. His energy and enthusiasm brought about the launch of London Weekend TV and later TVAM (he was one of the 'famous five' with Michael Parkinson, Angela Rippon, Anna Ford and Robert Key). My dealings with Mr Frost were minimal but he was keen to get me on board for his album which celebrated the American bi-centenary. Written and produced by Miki Anthony who had previously enjoyed minor success as a songwriter, artist and producer – the project was hopelessly ambitious although Mr Frost had invested heavily so I had to try – it eventually sank without a trace!

A rather more worthwhile investment from Mr Frost followed, a movie remake of the 'Cinderella' story, called 'The Slipper and the Rose' written by the legendary Sherman brothers whose previous work included 'Mary Poppins', 'Jungle Book' and 'Chitty Chitty Bang Bang'. I was to plug the soundtrack album and arrange for the sheet music to be printed and I was very proud of the results – so were the Shermans. The film was selected for a Royal Command Premier to be attended by the Queen and the Queen Mother but disappointingly, no invite for me!

During my 15 years at the company and as head of music, I was called upon to assess all kinds of extraordinary talent. I enjoyed a memorable evening watching Rowan Atkinson in a fringe theatre production, he performed a mime act which was brilliant but my report had to ask the question of how can we make a record with a silent artist? Actor Christopher Lee came by as he considered he was really cut out to be a singer so with the help of my flatmate producer, David Paramor we recorded a single at EMI – he was so loud the microphone was placed 20 feet away. The single was never released.

Radio 1 rock DJ, Tommy Vance was a little embarrassed to bring in a folk group from Manchester, The Fivepenny Piece but thought they had potential and they wrote their own songs. So, it was back to EMI whose A & R team suggested that in-house producer, Bob Barratt was perfect for them and without delay he recorded an album – a total of ten L.P.s were recorded and released in the following six years. The most successful, *King Cotton* made the Top 10 in 1976 and sold over 100,000 copies.

The group became resident guests on Esther Rantzen's highly rated 'That's Life' TV show and performed regular sessions for Radio Two. As their 'go-to' person in the company, I made regular trips to their home town, Stalybridge near Manchester where they could easily sell out at The Free Trade Hall. Not really my type of music – northern dialect folk, but a huge commercial success nonetheless. Tommy was a happy man as he was given shares in a joint venture publishing company, Wednesday Music but once again, Richard Armitage was indifferent.

One of the newer operating agents at the company, Michael P Cohen was very involved in the cabaret scene and convince Armitage that his discoveries, Justin and Wilde would sell millions of records, so I was directed to attend one of their shows in a tacky Manchester night club. Sure enough it was a complete riot with hundreds of middle-aged ladies going crazy for them, after a few martinis.

But the music was pretty bland, mainly popular covers and in my view these audiences were just having a fun night out and were not serious record buyers. However, undaunted Michael P secured a deal with Pye Records and as (for reasons unknown), they seemed to like me, I was given the task of producing a single. I booked the best session musicians and had time at Pye's own studios where many a hit had been recorded (The Kinks, Sandie Shaw, Petula Clark etc etc). I chose a Bread/David Gates song, *Down On My Knees*, one of their few up-tempo titles that I thought would be radio friendly.

Justin and Wilde never had a hit although they later worked with established producer, John McLeod who had many so in the end, I was right the first time.

Although I really enjoyed my time making demos – a fast process with instant gratification, I never wanted to be a producer as it seemed to involve spending too much time in a darkened room and demanded endless patience.

So strangely I found myself once again at the controls to co-produce (with Armitage's son but a much nicer man, Charles) the French legend, Claude Francois. The album was never completed, barely started in fact, due to his untimely death at the age of just 39 in 1978! One Saturday night I received a telephone call from his assistant in Paris informing me that Claude had been electrocuted while fixing a light bulb in his bathroom – bizarrely I was in the bath at the time of the call!

At this time, I was reaching the end of my career with Noel Gay and Charles Armitage was being groomed as my replacement. The company had taken on UK representation for Claude and arranged a concert at the Royal Albert Hall in a bid to increase his popularity here. Although the concert attracted over 6000 they were predominately French so it had a minimal effect on his British popularity. Claude decided the best way forward was to record an album totally in the English language as he also had his sights on American success. He did have a minor chart success here a couple of years earlier with *Tears On The Telephone* (ironic) but this was seen as something of a one-off.

After hanging out with Claude in London for a while, Charles and I became very friendly with him and he liked our energy and enthusiasm plus knowledge of contemporary music. Someone like Norman Newell would have been a more obvious choice of producer having had considerable success in this field but Claude just thought he was too old school. I was honest with him about my production capability (or lack of it) but his theory was if we hired the best and most expensive musicians, studios (in fact the esteemed Morgan Studios in Willesden, North London) and engineers, as a team we could get a good result.

The first song we recorded was written by Eddie Pumer whose band Fairfield Parlour (originally Kaleidoscope) had been on Noel Gay's roster but now Eddie had become a radio producer at London's Capital Radio. The band's most successful single was *Bordeaux Rose* which seemed an obvious choice being of all things – French but in fact very 'English' (everyone knows that the best Rose does not come from Bordeaux).

It was eventually released long after Claude's death but without success. While we pressed on with recording the album it became apparent that Claude's work ethic was pretty dismal – he would tire early in the studios and in our efforts to make him sound English so invited us to his resident table at Trader Vic's in London's Park Lane Hilton for cocktails. Then we had a long Christmas break – Claude had spoken at length about how much he was looking forward to uncorking a fine Chateau Lafite Rothschild from his well-stocked cellar as part of his family celebrations back in Paris.

When he returned to London to resume work on the album I asked how it went – "Catastrophe, the wine was corked!"

Claude had known incredible success in France, his country of residence (he was born in Egypt), achieving over 100 hit singles, all sung in French, all very cheesy and none of which charted in the UK. He was also a very gifted songwriter – most famously he wrote the original version of *My Way (Comme d'habitude)* with English lyrics by Paul Anka, one of the biggest songs of all time, Frank Sinatra recording the definitive version but others included Elvis Presley! There is no doubt that Claude had a wonderful, if far too short, life and I found him to be a very generous and likable man.

Claude Francoise – French superstar, over 70 million record sales

One of my ambitions for Noel Gay Music was to appoint a strong network of sub-publishers throughout the world and following around eight trips to the MIDEM festival in Cannes, I felt this had been achieved. The most important territory of course was the USA and as I have mentioned, doing business with Bob Reno and Eddie O'Loughlin was massively fruitful. One of the smaller but competitive territories was South Africa and there is no doubt that Clive Calder and his Music piece company led the way. Clive was also a big fan of Gary Benson's songs so wanted to do a deal. Clive and his partner Ralph Simon were generally on a charm offensive to secure representation of UK publishers and it certainly worked. Over time I found it strange that Clive and Ralph should visit London so regularly, given the relatively small amount of royalties involved coming out of their own market. They invited me to lunch/dinner on several occasions – eventually it came to light that they wanted as much information as possible about the UK music business as they intended to set up a London based company. Clive was always pleasant and charming but he was not always comfortable in a crowd (he had to leave the MPA Christmas lunch early with some form of claustrophobia) and suffered from several allergies! However, he was an interesting man and good company so I was happy to hang out with him especially as he also represented State Music where at the time Gary Benson was signed as an artist. It was obvious that Clive and Ralph were desperate to get out of South Africa as he saw no future there with their oppressive apartheid laws, quite apart from there being such a small music market.

Never one to miss a trick, during one MIDEM I bumped into Clive outside the (old) Palais de Festival and he asked if he could borrow my ID pass to gain entry I said "but you don't look anything like me not to mention that I need the pass myself as I was about to enter."

"No problem," he said, "they won't have time to check the photo and once I'm in I will throw the pass back to you out of the side window."

He obviously had thought this through and it all worked – so he saved around the equivalent of 500 Euros, a drop in the ocean when we look at what was to come!

In 1975 they set up Zomba Management in London, initially just representing record producer, Mutt Lange and singer, Richard Jon Smith from Cape Town – from these small beginnings came a giant, over time they had a grip on the world market. Mutt Lange soon became the hottest producer in town making the first Boomtown Rats, Graham Parker and AC/DC's massive 'Highway To Hell' albums. Def Leppard, Foreigner and Bryan Adams soon followed. I recall that before this Clive was offered an exclusive deal with Virgin Records for Mutt to make six albums a year for very good money and he asked my advice. My immediate thought was, *why lock into an exclusive deal when Mutt had the potential to record for just about any major label!* Clive took my advice but it was only Ralph who ever acknowledged my input.

Clive and Ralph soon set up a record company and enjoyed a string of UK hits on their label, Jive Records starting with a group made up of session singers, actors – Tight Fit, then A Flock Of Seagulls, before the more credible pop artist, Billy Ocean too the label to another level. This led to them opening their New York office and they set up a distribution deal with the mighty Clive Davies of

Arista Records. Around this time Clive discovered young whiz kid A & R man, Barry Weiss who specialised in hip hop and soon spotted the potential in this area enjoying hits with DJ Jazzy Jeff, A Tribe Called Quest, and the hugely successful R Kelly. Zomba fast became a major worldwide force going on to sign Britney Spears, Backstreet Boys, NSYNC whilst back in the UK, the label now run by my old friend, Steve Jenkins reverted to the pop market with Samantha Fox and Steps.

In the mid-1990s, Ralph parted company with Clive and went on to hold senior positions with Capitol and Blue Note Records as well as heading up Rondor Music in London (appointing Sharp End as promotion consultants), before forming Your Mobile and is currently president of Mobilium Global Ltd!

His settlement with Zomba was never disclosed but every time I see him he is smiling, so I guess he was happy with whatever it was... however the combination of sound business sense and an intuitive flair for music, resulted in a record breaking coup for Clive after BMG had purchased 25% of the company in which the deal contained a 'put option' meaning that if Zomba reached certain sales targets they had to buy the remaining shares at a very high multiple, if Clive exercised this option. In 2002 we saw the net result which was a figure of 2.74 billion dollars – the highest purchase figure in the history of the business.

The feeling within the business was that Clive was so obsessed with the music game, he would carry on and perhaps even buy the (by then) troubled EMI.

As far as I can tell, Clive has just vanished – yes, it does seem that he took the money and ran but good luck to him.

CLIVE CALDER – arguably the most successful music business executive ever, I knew him at the very beginning through the '70s and early '80s playing a small but significant part of his success, without numeration.

RALPH SIMON

RALPH SIMON – partner in the Zomba group since its inception for over 20 years. Still very active, now in the mobile entertainment business.

I had been tempted to resign my position at Noel Gay in 1969 when work colleagues, David Enthoven and John Gaydon had discovered King Crimson so left the company to set up EG Records and management. They invited me to an early Crimson rehearsal at a small studio in the Fulham Road, West London, where they played the most dynamic set I had ever heard – they just blew me away. David and John offered me a job to do their promotion and run their publishing company. I was sorely tempted having seen the band play live at the Ewell Tech College and then again at the Rolling Stones free Hyde Park concert. The guys also offered me a soft option which was for me to sign their publishing to Noel Gay so I could handle the album promo anyway, but they wanted a small advance. Small but big enough that I had to clear it with Armitage – he hit the roof, angry that David and John had left the company and were cheeky enough to look for money. This outcome was a huge personal disappointment but I decided to stay loyal to the company for a while longer – I was just not ready.

'In The Court of The Crimson King' iconic album cover.
The publishing was so nearly mine.

In fact, it was another nine years before I finally decided to move on, shortly after the huge success with John Travolta in America, which made me realise I really could generate success under my own steam and I now had the confidence that I could do it for myself. It was a major move after 15 years of security (salary, expenses and company car) but the financial offer I received from Bob Reno and Eddie O'Loughlin's Midsong International was a big enough compensation. It also gave me the opportunity to realise the dream of being independent, continue working with Gary Benson and most of all working with my friend Eddie O'Loughlin.

Eddie O'Loughlin, David Mindel and Phillip Kruse
(Norwegian subpublisher and friend). MIDEM 2012.

Chapter 2
RMO Music Publishing

On the first of January 1979, I officially opened my own office in Alfred Place, just off London's Tottenham Court Road with my PA from Noel Gay, Jayne Edwards as the only other member of staff (Bob Reno was a 'sleeping partner'). I was sub-letting two rooms from a friend, a one-time employee of my old sheet music printers and the location was just a short walk to the BBC's Broadcasting House, so I was all set to go.

I had already had Gary Benson on my roster but it was essential to build a strong publishing catalogue by exclusively signing many more songwriters. Previous associations came into play: I had met Eddie Hardin, former Spencer Davis vocalist, in a Hamburg club when he was touring as Hardin/York (Pete York was Spencer's drummer) and now he had formed a new band, Axis Point with Charlie Whitney (ex-Family guitarist) – they had a record deal with RCA but were looking for a publisher. After a few pub sessions and the payment of a reasonable advance, the deal was mine.

Another former contact, record producer/musician, Tony Cox and his wife, singer-songwriter, Lesley Duncan also came on board. Aura Records' Aaron Sixx was quick to make contact – as his artist, jazz/art rock singer, Annette Peacock was looking for a deal and finally yet another singer songwriter, Hratch was signed – I had the foundations of a great catalogue.

My new partner, Bob Reno brought in the Spelling Goldberg TV music catalogue to the table on a UK admin deal – titles included were from Starsky and Hutch, Charlie's Angels, Love Boat, Fantasy Island and many more Hollywood productions, a real money spinner.

In addition to the Reno funding, I obtained substantial advances from sub-publishers from all over the world, negotiated at the MIDEM music festival later that month (full story on that event later).

I also had a rather beneficial arrangement with Pete Waterman and David Howells who had started Miracle Records (Pete's rather misguided slogan was 'If it's a hit, it's a miracle'), whereby they would secure publishing rights for

RMO in return for my plugging services. Only one release did any business – Patsy Gallant's *0 Michel* as she came in for some promo, but the idea was well intended (and was repeated with rather more success a few years later).

Eddie O'Loughlin had a similar idea with Sharon Brown's *I Specialise In Love* on the hot Virgin Records label and was a Top 40 hit in the UK.

Sharon Brown's hit single, produced by Eddie O'Loughlin.

Patsy Gallant's single on Pete Waterman's first record label, Miracle.

Generally everything was running pretty well for the first two years but I had underestimated the huge costs in running a company with a West End office and I had incurred massive legal fees in getting all these various contracts signed. All was OK until, without notice, Spelling Goldberg cancelled the admin deal in order to take a substantial advance from a major publisher, Warner-Chappell.

Then fate played its part – back at MIDEM in January 1981, I bumped into an old plugging friend, Roger Bolton in the Carlton Hotel rest rooms. Immediately he asked me if I wanted a job running Bron's music division (he was head of promotion for the record label, Bronze). My immediate response was to decline and tell him I was happy with running my own company. However, back in London talks continued with the owner, Gerry Bron who seemed determined to get me on board. In the end it was an offer I could not refuse as benefits included, overheads being covered (as I would be based in their Chalk Farm premises) they would pay my PA Jayne's salary as well as mine ;. they would administer my catalogue for a minimal 15 per cent ; I could run RMO alongside the impressive Bron Publishing and they would provide me with a company car plus pay all my expenses.

I was still slightly reluctant having become accustomed to being free and independent but this idea appeared to offer up the welcome comfort of financial security. There was other news which made things decisive – my friend Eddie O'Loughlin had left Midsong International (to launch his own company, Next Plateau) and Bob Reno himself had gone missing in LA!

Chapter 3
Bron Music Publishing / Bronze Records

Three months later, immediately after the April, 1981 Easter break, with all contracts signed I started my new role as General Manager at Bron Music which boasted some great evergreen songs including *God Bless The Child*, *At The Hop*, *Dance On*, *Ha Ha Said The Clown*, and many of Gene Pitney's hits. But the big earners were now from the record label's roster of rock bands including Uriah Heep, Manfred Mann's Earth Band, Motorhead and Girlschool! The company was originally set up by Sydney Bron, another Tin Pan Alley man with his son, Gerry opening up the record company subsidiary and producing many of their albums. The publishing company also represented some highly successful writers including Tony Hazzard, Richard Myhill and Mike Heron from the Incredible String Band. Other assets included the Roundhouse recording studios and an agency division run by top executive, Neil Warnock. It seemed like the perfect set up to me and I was full of optimism regarding my future. I sailed through the first year enjoying the support and company of some great colleagues.

Motorhead enjoyed their first No 1 album and some exciting new signings came along with The Damned and Sundance, fronted by Mary Hopkin and produced by husband Tony Visconti. What could possibly go wrong?

However, when my friend at RCA, Shaun Greenfield suggested I was offered the publishing on Scottish band, H2O there was a dilemma, a potential conflict of interests! Do I take it for my own RMO Music or sign it to Bron – I decided to front out Gerry thinking he would not be interested as they were looking for a £2000 advance. Of course, I was wrong, they had a record deal and would easily recoup this amount, so I was obliged to put it into Bron.

Initially I loved being involved with H20 and working with Shaun plus we brought in another close colleague, Tony Cox to produce the album. The first song we completed was *Dream To Sleep* which went on to be a hit and the band secured a support slot on Kajagoogoo's sell out UK tour. Before I knew it I was being drawn into the management role which involved several trips to their

Glasgow base as well as countless gigs. It is par for the course that when the follow up fails the blame game starts. However, the adventure continued into the next phase of my career – more of that later.

Meanwhile, Tony Cox brought in an amazing three-piece band, The Mechanics and after checking them out live with record company boss, Robert Lemon, they were signed to the label. Their first single, *The Power Of Love* attracted massive Radio 1 airplay and the band played an 'In Concert' special, hosted by the legendary John Peel. In spite of all this activity Gerry was not impressed by the figures – sales vs costs were in the negative.

I had noticed that Gerry was generally distracted away from the music and it finally became apparent that he was focusing on building an airline of all things.

I was banking huge cheques coming in from Bron's sub-publishers – Germany was particularly lucrative and we had finalised a new deal for the future catalogue with international major publishers, Intersong bringing in a very large advance.

The nature of my RMO admin deal was for Bron to collect the royalties and pay out my and the writers share to me every quarter. Year two, month three a statement arrived but no cheque. I did nothing. Year two, month six – a repeat so I had to take action as I was having to pay out my writers without receiving anything from Bron.

By this time and most fortuitously I had become very friendly with record company boss, Robert Lemon and over lunch one day he revealed the company was in serious financial difficulty as all the money was going into the airline and the airline was failing! For a few months we tried to ride out the storm but started to discuss alternative plans, just in case. Then the time came, Robert was made redundant so the game was up.

So much for financial security – I was left being owed over £30,000 in royalties and as is the way they go, the creditors meeting concluded that there was no money to pay any of the creditors – the largest being Manfred Mann whose band had sold millions all over the world. My parting encounter with Gerry was quite amicable (from his side) and he offered me his Daimler Sovereign as that was all he had.

Fortunately, by then Robert and I had developed our plan and had already sourced office premises in Soho's Golden Square, commenced the then notoriously long procedure in having a telephone connected, ordered the furniture and agreed with my new PA, Sue Foster to join us in our new venture – to be named R & R Music.

PUBLISHING

Ron + Bron deal working out

RON McCREIGHT has been running Bron Music, plus his own RMD Publishing in tandem, for nine months now, and doesn't regret deciding to combine the roles.

The nine-month gestation is also leading to the birth of useful new copyrights by the signing of new writing talent. And McCreight is paying special attention to writers capable of penning generally exploitable songs as well as those locked into specific bands with particular identities, whose work does not lend itself normally to covers.

He mentioned in this connection Richard Myhill, who has penned What's Love for Sundance, the Mary Hopkin Mike Hurst group signed by Bronze Records. He rates Myhill as "contemporary in the widest sense of the word" and ideal for both Bron Music and Bronze Records "which are in no way limited to a narrow musical outlook".

Nick Dickman is another writer with considerable potential in McCreight's estimation. Dickman from North Wales is writing for Bronze band Small Ads, and has "refreshing originality about his work, which is modern but humorous".

McCreight has a well established catalogue at his disposal in Bron Music, ranging from the Max Bygraves hit You're A Pink Toothbrush today enjoying another lease of profitable life via The Smurfs through Listen To Me (recorded by The Hollies) and Dance On (The Shadows) to the Billie Holiday classic God Bless The Child.

"Any publisher with a catalogue of hits going back 20 years or more is obviously having a very good run at the moment with the advent of what I call the exploiting medley, TV compilations and budget albums. We're working the catalogue, but where are the standards of tomorrow?"

With 15 years at the publishing wing of the Noel Gay Organisation before founding his own RMD enterprise and then combining with Bron, McCreight has acquired a perceptive overview of the publishing scene in general, particularly in these times of recession.

"The problem to some extent is the major record companies relying totally on young A&R men, who are very good in the field, but don't have the breadth of vision to recognise the seeds of something on a tape in the office.

"I'll go to anyone I think may be interested in the material I have to offer as long as I feel they have an appreciation and understanding of it."

Helping him in his activities are James Bestwick, royalty and copyright manager, and promotion man Roger Bolton. And there's the redoubtable founder of the business, Sydney Bron now 60 but still putting in four days a week.

RON McCREIGHT: no regrets

Cuban wins Yamaha song fest

TOKYO: Osvaldo Rodriguez of Cuba won the 12th Popular Song Festival organised by the Yamaha Music Foundation here. Digamos Que Mas Da (Let's Say What More It Matters), with music by Mind). Rodriguez, blind from birth, composed and performed the winning song.

The first prize for Japanese entries went to Aled, a nine-strong rock group from Nagoya, with The Inner Rock 'n' Roller written and lead singer Shigeru Takahara.

Best song awards went to Peaches & Herb, Bucks Fizz (UK), and Togni (Italy), and Viyakarn (Thailand). Sel (Mexico) and Juergens (Austria) won outstanding performer awards.

Just one year before the collapse of the Bron Organisation a positive feature in Music Week magazine.

Chapter 4
R & R Music and Management/
R4 Records / Legend Records

Not only did we have an office ready to go but I had taken with me the management of H20 who were still successfully touring and had their first album due for release on RCA. Robert brought in guitarist Snowy White who had played with Pink Floyd and Thin Lizzy and had a deal with Towerbell Records.

Also I was able to reclaim my original RMO publishing catalogue and transferred all the copyrights into the brand new R & R Music.

Although we had an income stream from the publishing and management commission from our two artists, in retrospect we were always going to be financially venerable running such an ambitious set up.

Snowy had a big hit with his *Bird Of Paradise* but then his label went out of business; H2O came up with a worthy follow up their hit, *Dream To Sleep* in 'Just Outside Of Heaven' but even after an intense plugging exercise it peaked at No 38.

Robert (Lemon) enjoyed artists' management but was more comfortable in running a record company so we set up R4 Records, securing a distribution deal with EMI and of course our first release was Snowy's follow up *For You*.

This move exposed us even further when it came to finance – with the video alone costing £15,000 which was the going rate in those days. We also funded Snowy's album and being perfectionists, it proved a hugely expensive record.

Although our publishing income covered our basic overheads, the record label was a reckless gamble – we also signed indie bands The Higsons and The Larks plus another Scottish band, Pure Glass who were seriously good musicians with a soul/funk vibe.

In retrospect we were absolutely crazy!

We really gambled everything on Snowy's new single and ran a phenomenal campaign on radio, TV, press, retail and general marketing. We worked it so incredibly hard but after several weeks it finally just peaked at No 65. Although he had a tour to support the album release, we really needed the single to take off in order to sell some albums.

Meanwhile we had also set up a tour for H20 including a London show at London's Pheonix Theatre and we even organised coach transport for their fan club to attend, ensuring a sell-out. We took up our seats that night full of pride and optimism but once the band started we felt uncomfortable – there was something wrong. Singer, Ian Donaldson did his best to conceal a throat infection but his performance was well below par – back stage the band were in pieces! With fifteen more dates to come, I sourced the best throat specialist in Harley Street whose claim to fame was removing Ringo Starr's tonsils. Ian's treatment was only partly successful so was only able to complete two more shows, then we had to cancel. Thankfully we had insured the tour!

RCA continued to support us and the band so we carried on. Nonetheless it really was problem after problem and I seemed to spend most of my time flying to Glasgow to resolve their issues, with the city's Holiday Inn becoming my second home. Their exceptional live shows helped us keep the faith but, H2O were proving just to be big trouble. One particular Edinburgh show ended prematurely in a mass brawl so I made a quick exit; another was memorable for all the wrong reasons – a sell-out Friday night show attracted several executives from RCA flying up to check it out. At the advance party, I called their tour manager as soon as I landed at Edinburgh airport –

"A slight problem," he reported, "Kenny the drummer is in hospital!"

I diverted to the local A and E department to see Kenny lying there covered in plaster – apparently he had dashed out of the rehearsals to buy cigarettes, attempting to catch the shop before closing and was knocked down by a car. At first he defiantly insisted he could go ahead with the gig but there was no doubt we had to cancel. Now it fell to me to break the bad news to the mass gathering from the record company. I sheepishly walked into the hotel bar – it seemed everyone was very excited to be there so I had to explain immediately.

I just went for it – "Sorry guys but Kenny has had an accident, and is in hospital so the gig is cancelled."

They hardly drew breath other than to offer me a drink and were almost dismissive about missing the show, they were just happy to be there for a nice dinner and a general 'jolly' on expenses!

H20's only album for RCA. There was considerable deliberation about using lead singer, Ian Donaldson's picture on the front cover but the marketing department thought we should take advantage of his strong image, causing a major internal dispute within the band.

I was rapidly coming to the conclusion that management was not for me although Robert still enjoyed it especially as a solo artist and a really nice one at that did not present the problems of a six piece from Glasgow. I happily carried on with running our publishing company but the record label was a constant drain on our resources.

On a more positive note, we were making waves within the business and we were on the radar of former Warner Records MD, Mike Heap. He had recently left the major and raised funding from an investment company, Prestwich Holdings in order to start his own label, but he wanted partners so had approached us. Appreciating our ability to run companies, having a well located London base and liking the idea of representing Snowy and H20, we were his perfect allies. Mike intended to add Elkie Brooks to the roster.

It all seemed absolutely perfect but the deal was one of the most stressful and lengthy negotiations I had ever experienced. Being in such an obviously weak position the Prestwich guys were making so many unreasonable demands and continually threatening to pull out – but we really were desperate. To his credit, Mike was determined to make it happen, so after four months of negotiation, finally it did, and Legend Records was born.

Throughout this period of completion, we were running up more and more debts including huge legal fees, so in the end the proceeds from the sale of R & R / R 4 only just covered our liabilities. However we did have a new well-funded company to run with good salaries, company cars and expenses so we set about this new adventure with renewed energy and enthusiasm.

Elkie Brooks was duly signed and became our absolute priority. Top producer-songwriter, Russ Ballard (also founder member of The Roulettes and Argent) was commissioned to make the album and he came up with a gem in *No More The Fool* which was the first single. The promotion campaign was one of the most extensive and intense I had ever encountered with high pressure coming from Elkie, Mike and the all-powerful execs at Prestwich! She was considered very TV friendly so we did well in securing several prime time slots but Radio 1 airplay, as ever, was a problem.

However, Elkie imposed very strict conditions upon every single radio and TV appearance including one of us driving to Paddington station to meet her every time she travelled from her Devon home. She eventually revealed that she was pregnant so her demands were not that unreasonable after all.

Elkie Brooks album released November 1986 on Legend Records and reaching No five in the UK charts.

My first experience of Elkie was at Ronnie Scott's club in London's Soho where she performed with Robert Palmer as Vinegar Joe. I was instantly captivated by her powerful, soulful vice – little did I know then what was to come.

Following the duo going their own separate ways, Elkie was picked up by one of my old plugging friends, Derek Green who was then UK MD of A and M Records. Derek was one of the great A & R men of that generation and his expert guidance made her a star. Derek found some wonderful songs including *Lilac Wine*, *Don't Cry Out Loud*, *Pearl's A Singer* and *Sunshine After The Rain* with producers such as the legends, Leiber and Stoller (with whom I worked with later). Although she had an amazing long run of success, when her record sales went into decline and, as is often the case, she became disillusioned with the record business and not unreasonably developed a mistrust of us executives. Along with Mike Heap and Robert, I tried to rebuild some trust – in part I think we were successful and we all enjoyed a highly successful campaign with her appearances on TV shows such as Wogan, Des O'Connor Tonight, Pebble Mill and finally 'Top of the Pops' plus eventually airplay from Radio 1's 'A list', the *No More The Fool* single reached No Five in the UK singles chart with the album peaking at exactly the same number.

It was not unusual for Elkie's husband, Trevor to make an appearance in our office to offer his advice. A sound engineer from the live circuit where they had met on one of her many tours. Likeable but rather obsessive, Trevor has been known to turn up at a TV or radio show with his own microphone as he considered the BBC's equipment not being up to his high standards. With Elkie finally giving birth over that Christmas break, she was right back with us to make her 'Top of the Pops' appearance and to continue with the promotion trail. We arranged a nationwide radio promotion tour as at that time all the big cities had their own major commercial radio station. I was volunteered to start things off and flew to Edinburgh with Elkie, the baby and her nanny, rented a car on arrival and set off to Radio Forth for the first interview. We were on schedule for the interview but we had a forced stop with the baby screaming for food – we missed our live slot which I considered unprofessional so suddenly we had an unhappy ship. Fortunately, I was able to persuade the radio producer to pre-record an interview which would go to air later. Then we set off to Glasgow and to Radio Clyde, back on schedule. However, Elkie was now hungry so a lunch-stop and more screaming from the baby, heavy traffic, so seriously delayed I had to drive like a maniac to make it on time! We made it so in the end a successful day with two major radio stations covered and we then headed for the tranquillity of my second home, the Holiday Inn, Glasgow for a nice dinner and some rest. After this experience I called in a professional 'road manager' to take over in Manchester so the next day I made sure the Elkie part boarded the plane and I head back to London. However, I did have to re-join them in Birmingham for the Pebble Mill TV show but this was comparably an easy job.

Unfortunately, the follow up singles, both covers *We've Got Tonight* (Bob Seger) and *Only Women Bleed* (Alice Cooper) did not perform well which made for the beginning of the end for Elkie and indeed Legend Records itself after just over a year of trading. It later transpired that Prestwich were only in the game for a 'quick buck' and just kept all the income from Elkie's album which they later sold to Polydor for £500,000. Their position was that Legend's other releases failed and *No More The Fool* only just broke even – indeed we found out later that they deducted all the recording, marketing and promotion costs from Elkie's royalties leaving her in debt! Robert and I couldn't help but feel used!

Twenty-three years later I was reunited with Elkie to plug her 'Powerless' album for Right Track Records in 2009. Although not reaching the heights of our Legend release, it performed well and she sang live on Jools Holland's Radio Two show from the iconic BBC Maida Vale studios. Husband Trevor failed to show up with his microphone.

It is a great testament to Elkie's staying power that in 2017 she made it back on to the Radio Two playlist with *Love Aint Something You Get For Free*, taken from a compilation of hits and a few new songs. In 2018 she was back again on national TV, 'The One Show' performing *Running From the Future* from the 'Finding Your Feet' movie. As I write, Elkie is still planning just one more 'farewell tour' at the age of 76.

Meanwhile, Robert and I had to start yet again but at least we had retained the lease on our Golden Square offices and cleared our debts, so we looked forward with optimism.

So in the summer of 1987 we brainstormed ideas and came up with by far the best yet – an independent promotion/PR company serving the industry and having spent most of my career so far plugging our own records, I felt well equipped to take this on, but for who?

Chapter 5
Sharp End Promotions

Robert and I did not get too far with our list of potential clients – our brain storming started with the names of Pete Waterman and David Howells, both of whom I had known for much of my 25 year career and following the success of some early productions, written and recorded by Stock, Aitken, Waterman (including Dead or Alive, Mel and Kim, Hazel Dean and Princess) had decided to launch their own PWL Records!

The stars were certainly aligned – we walked into to the PWL offices and studios in the Borough (near London Bridge), at exactly the right time. Pete and David were keen to play us two singles, *Never Gonna Give You Up* by Rick Astley and *Roadblock* by SAW themselves to demonstrate what they could do. Listening to Rick's single was a defining moment, I had never heard such a brilliant pop record ever before. We could almost smell the hits that were yet to come although these singles were already licensed out – Rick to RCA and SAW to A and M.

During the meeting we described our ambition to be the best promotion company in the business and how we would thrive on being at the 'Sharp End' – "That's what you call the company kid!" said Pete.

So Sharp End Promotions was formed at the end of 1987 and over the next five years it represented over 100 'Top 40 hits' including 15 'No 1 singles' and six 'No 1 albums'.

Company directors / shareholders were myself, Robert Lemon, Pete Waterman and David Howells. Staff comprised my former secretary, Sue Foster (who had remained loyal from the Bronze disaster through R & R and Legend, gaining huge experience along the way) and later we were joined by Australian, Liz Watson to handle TV and Maria Philippou for regional – the 'A' team was then complete.

Sue, Liz, Maria, Robert and Ron – the 'A' team 1987–2005

Our work ethic was extremely high – there was no choice with so many artists appearing on so multiple TV and radio shows, plus countless press interviews and photo calls. 'Top of the Pops' alone involved a considerable amount of planning, organising stage plans, choreography and call sheets. However, we thrived on the challenge and also made time to celebrate every success in style.

In terms of single releases, we had a rather low key start with Mandy Smith's *I Just Can't Wait* only creeping into the Top 100 singles. It seemed that the idea was to capitalise on her notorious relationship and subsequent marriage to Bill Wyman but sadly UK record sales were minimal although Mandy did breakthrough in Germany and Scandinavia.

The best was most definitely yet to come but as with many great things it was almost an accident! *I Should Be So Lucky* by Kylie Minogue was a record that Pete was reluctant to make but became the biggest single of 1988 and put her, as well as Sharp End, well and truly on the map. The full Kylie story follows later, but her breakthrough marked the beginning of an unprecedented run of hits with Jason Donovan close behind, followed by Sinitta, Sonia, Hazel Dean, Sybil, Brother Beyond, Angry Anderson, Big Fun, Samantha Fox, Pat 81 Mick, 2 Unlimited and later from outside of the PWL stable, Danni Minogue, Take That, Boyzone, N-Trance, Yell, Shakin' Stevens, Leo Sayer, Petula Clark, Tom Jones, George Benson, Dionne Warwick, Jennifer Paige, John Alford, Nicki French, etc.

Sharp End became the most successful independent promotion/PR company in the history of the music industry and in its original form ran out the hits for 15 glorious years!

MUSIC WEEK MAGAZINE AD – September 1991. Sharp End published its own chart of 75 hits in four years – unprecedented.

On the 'best things happen by accident' theme, we originally had no intention of setting up a press division but in the all-out effort to get Kylie into the charts, we would sit around with Pete making up stories for all the tabloid press but the only person to do the leg work at the time was our Sue. It was impressive how quickly she rose to the job and established solid relationships with all the columnists and editors – pretty soon the work involved keeping Kylie out of the papers as it was they making up the stories. As the work load increased we employed Liz which seemed natural being Australian with our top two artists both coming from Melbourne – the second being Jason Donovan. In his own controversial style, Pete most definitely did NOT want Jason on the label – "No more soap stars kid!"

He was signed to Kylie's Australian label, Mushroom with whom PWL MD David Howells had locked in with a reciprocal record and publishing deal. David felt obliged to take on Jason so arranged a meeting with him and manager, Richard East in London on a 'Neighbours' plugging trip. Robert and I immediately warmed to Jason and went to see him being interviewed on the Wogan TV show staged in the Shepherds Bush Empire where the atmosphere was electric – the audience went ballistic as soon as he came on stage and it was obvious to us that he would be a massive pop star. We went back to Pete in an attempt to persuade him – he showed us the door in no uncertain terms! The happy 'accident' here was in Rick Astley refusing to vocalise a new SAW song, 'Nothing Can Divide Us' – Pete called asking if Jason was still in town – luckily he was, so we rapidly drove him down to the Borough studios and the result was his first hit, reaching No Five in September 1988.

In the meantime, our workload had become almost overwhelming – we had worked on Kylie's follow up, *Got To Be Certain*, Sinitta's *GTO* and *Cross My Broken Heart*, Hazell Dean's come-back single, *Who's Leaving Who* (which became her biggest hit ever) and a cover of *Let's All Chant* recorded by Capital Radio DJs Pat Sharp and Mick Brown in aid of the station's 'Help A London Child' fundraiser staged every Easter. It was at this point we brought in Maria but we also had help from Pete himself! Between us we set up an evening for some top Radio 1 producers to visit the PWL studios where Pete played the perfect host and played them the Hazell single before heading for the adjacent Gladstone pub. A good time was had by all and the record was soon added to the Radio 1 A-list! Every one really was a winner and it seemed everything that SAW produced, turned to gold.

Not everything automatically went onto the PWL label – for political reasons, Sonia was licenced to Chrysalis Records (A & R man Peter Robinson had previously picked up the Rick Astley deal when at RCA), Big Fun were already signed to Jive, Brother Beyond to EMI and Sinitta to Simon Cowell's Fanfare Records.

Sonia had the most infectious personality and had gate crashed Pete's radio show in her home town of Liverpool (194 Radio City) for an impromptu audition. This was Pete at his best, spotting the potential in a loveable 'scouser' and inspiring Matt and Mike to write a Number One song in *You'll Never Stop Me Loving You*.

As part of the promotion campaign, Sonia appeared at the Radio One roadshow when it visited her nearby location of Southport. In most cases for technical reasons artists would mime to their hit but there was always a challenge put out by producers for them to sing live – they had their way with Sonia and although she was brilliant, immediately following her performance I received from David Howells complaining that Mike Stock had heard it and was horrified by the sound and considered this would kill the sales! We rode the storm and the record went to No 1 selling over 400,000.

Chapter 6
Simon Cowell

From music business hopeful to world domination – quite unbelievable!

With the fast developing success of Sharp End at this time, it was becoming increasingly obvious that Simon wanted to join our club as he desperately needed to build his reputation and make a success of his Fanfare Records. Things had started well with Simon convincing Pete to produce a few tracks with Sinitta resulting in a string of hits for her – he also wanted Sharp End in to plug her records as her first single, *So Macho* had been ignored by Radio 1.

His next project was boy duo, Yell who ticked all the pop boxes and came up with a strong track in *Instant Replay*, produced by Nigel Wright and mixed by PWL's Pete Hammond. At a planning meeting, Simon enquired about TV possibilities – we ran out a list of around 30 possible shows, most of which we had just secured for Sonia. As was often his way, Simon was in disbelief but we delivered most of the shows we listed for Yell and the record reached No 10 without significant airplay. The entire concept of music on TV was his alert into many other opportunities which of course continues to this day. This came too late for Fanfare and the company collapsed – Simon moved on to RCA/BMG with his own imprint, S Records.

First of all, he was fastest to react to Robson and Jerome's big TV moment when they performed *Unchained Melody* in their hit TV series, 'Soldier, Soldier'. The single went to No 1 and there it stayed for seven weeks – it was also voted the worst single of 1995 by NME readers. However, this did not prevent single sales of 1.8 million and two further No 1 singles and albums. However, controversy seemed to follow any success Simon enjoyed and there was bad press surrounding the duo, throwing doubt into who was actually singing on their records (they were 'assisted' by session singers). Now learning fast, Simon developed other TV characters such as Zig and Zag, The Power Rangers, the Teletubbies, WWF and then he landed The Woolpackers and their line dancing album in our laps!

Before he finally enjoyed all this success, there were many desperate times for Mr Cowell as, after a string of hits, Sinitta's career had faltered and his frustration once spilled over during a 'Top of the Pops' rehearsal. Being somewhat opinionated, Simon had objected to Sinitta's choice of costume and with this artist being no pushover, things became loud and emotional until I broke up the argument taking him out of the studio and suggesting he did not return so we could get the show done without further drama.

Simon's partner in Fanfare Records was Iain Burton who now runs his own luxury brand, Aspinal and at the time it seemed he was responsible for funding the label. In truth it was doubtful that the funds were sufficient to cover the company's overhead, recording costs and their extravagant lifestyles. Although they had the hit with Yell, other such as Cousin Rachel were miserable and expensive failures. In 2011 I was interviewed by Tom Bower, author of 'Sweet Revenge', the most recent Cowell biography and in this I described a live TV performance by the girl/boy duo when the boy's hat fell off, he stopped to pick it up and the choreography broke down – a total embarrassment.

Tom Boyer describes: "With Sinitta's future in doubt Cowell casually began searching for new artists. Inevitably, he sought advice from Ron McCreight – 'getting pop played on Radio 1 is a nightmare', McCreight confessed, 'even Kylie is ignored'." ********

The publicist's salvation was television shows. He frequently accompanied Kylie Minogue to TV studios and was bemused by how often Cowell tagged along to meet the producers, using the opportunity to promote artists such as Cousin Rachel. After considerable effort, McCreight arranged for them to appear live on Saturday morning television. Cowell carefully choreographed their dance routine and dictated their clothes, including a hat for the boy. Watching the programme at home, Cowell saw the hat fall off and the performance collapse into chaos.

"A fucking disaster," he told McCreight.

"You chose what they should wear," replied McCreight.

"Another punt that's gone wrong!"

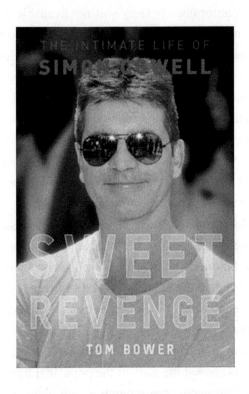

Sweet Revenge by Tom Boyer; published by Faber and Faber, copyright 2012

*********(re Kylie) not entirely accurate as although Kylie's first single was initially a struggle in obtaining Radio 1 airplay (Capital Radio played it from the start), thereafter every single was an automatic add to their playlist. In retrospect, it seems as if Sharp End was a major influence to moving the radio station back into playlist pop with Kylie at the heart of it. Radio 1's flagship summer roadshows were the platform for their audience to actually see their heroes and build bridges with the public generally. Initially the producers considered the DJs to be the stars and rejected the offer of booking major artists. Once we persuaded them to take Kylie on, her debut on a beach in Newquay brought in over 10,000 people and was an absolute sensation – there was no looking back for Radio 1 or Kylie.

In his relentless pursuit of success, Simon turned to his favourite Disney movie, 'The Jungle Book' and commissioned pop producer, Nigel Wright to record a medley of *Bare Necessities* and *I Wanna Be Like You* which went out under the name of The UK Mixmasters, featuring actor Gary Wilmot on vocals. Not an easy one to plug but we did manage to secure a slot on the all-important

'Top of the Pops' – unfortunately Gary was not available on the given date so Simon replaced him with session singer, Gary Martin who would sing live on the show. During rehearsals the TV producers received a letter from Wilmot's lawyer threatening legal action if the performance went ahead. We were summoned to the studio control room with Simon who contacted the BMG legal team – several heated conversations followed but finally it was agreed that the record company would indemnify the BBC against any possible action taken. After a long delay the rehearsals continued. The single made it into the Top 20 but was it worth it? Yet another example of how trouble seemed to follow him around but in our eyes, the worst was yet to come.

Once Simon had enjoyed such considerable success, particularly with Robson and Jerome, he seemed indestructible, except some venerability that came to light when he called me in to BMG offices for lunch (which turned out to be a cheese sandwich in the local cafe) – he had recently returned from their international conference where all the senior executives had criticised his roster for being only relevant in the UK.

Shortly after our meeting, he landed us with his next venture – The Woolpackers who comprised the stars of the popular 'Emmerdale' soap. Simon insisted that Sharp End handle the promotion and although the music was not exactly to our liking, there was no way of saying no! The only way to go with this project was, definitely not radio, once again TV was the only way – not really a problem as the Emmerdale cast were very well known in that world. The single 'Hillybilly Rock, Hillbilly Roll' was a huge success reaching No 5 in the UK but the parent album 'Emmer Dance' disappointingly peaked at No 26. As Simon had obtained a large marketing budget from BMG, this was not considered good enough and the blame was directed toward Sharp End. We were in a political crossfire as we were unaware of an unrelated dispute between Simon and Mike Stock and Matt Aitken who had now teamed up (without Pete) to form Love This Records. They had given Mr Cowell huge success in the expert production of the Robson and Jerome records but to this day, I don't know the background to the big fall out. Around the same time, Mike and Matt had secured Sharp End services for their label which started with a hit for Nicki French, with her cover of *Total Eclipse Of The Heart* achieving a Top 5 chart position in the UK but going all the way to No 2 in the USA. Now we were working their next signing, the star of TV's 'London's Burning', John Alford who Simon had turned down several months before. We had already secured the current BBC Saturday morning TV for the Woolpackers but ITV's 'Motormouth' were not keen. Then they called us requesting an appearance for John Alford which naturally we accepted. They also offered up a video showing for the Woolpackers as a gesture of good faith. Simon hit the roof and unreasonably accused us of favouritism – this proved to be the end of the road for us and the mighty Mr Cowell.

A sad ending but in the preceding years we had always enjoyed hanging out with Simon and he certainly knew how to celebrate success, even though much of it belonged to Sharp End and PWL! In retrospect it is easy to see that with his absolute determination and self-belief he would become a success but not to the level that he went on to achieve.

I met up with him again in 2015 at the Grosvenor House Hotel where he was being honoured by the Music Industry Trust for his 'contribution to music, entertainment and charitable causes' – not bad for someone who knows so little about music. But, good luck to him, he knew people that did, and in our chat he said "well we did have some fun!"

Chapter 7
Kylie Minogue

There is no doubt that Kylie would never had made it without the support of PWL and our PR company, Sharp End Promotions!

Shortly after opening the doors in Grafton House, David Howells pitched us the original Australian hit version of 'The Locomotion' but we were unsure of it's potential, especially given that Radio 1 at the time were still only playing rock music. Indeed, it had been shopped around the record labels who had all passed. However we immediately recognised Kylie's potential in the TV world so checked with the BBC press office about their plans for 'Neighbours' in the UK – good news, they were moving it from the 'dead' mid-morning slot, to lunchtime and early evenings to reach the children who would be home from school.

A few weeks later, David Howells had arranged with their Australian counterparts, Mushroom Records for Kylie to take a break from the TV show in order to visit London and make a record with SAW. We duly noted the date when it was announced at our weekly meeting, also attended by Pete Waterman.

When the day came, which happened to be another meeting day, I casually mentioned her impending arrival – Pete said, "NO, it's next week!" – He was wrong, he disappeared.

In support of David Howells endeavours, throughout the week we hung out with Kylie, her mother Carol and Mushroom boss, Gary Ashley while Matt and Mike started to come up with song ideas for her. Finally on that Friday, on her way back to Heathrow airport, Kylie arrived at the studios – reception called out – "Kylie is here for her session." – Overheard by club promo guy, Pitstop – "She should be so lucky,"… now there is a song idea. She put down her vocals on a basic rhythm track and returned to Melbourne – it was then put to one side for a while.

Some weeks later David Howells had a call from the then 'Top of the Pops' producer, Michael Hurll who was looking for an Australian artist for his 1987 Christmas morning BBC 1 TV special, traditionally hosted by Noel Edmunds.

Fortunately, Hurll was a frequent visitor to Australia and was vaguely aware of Kylie – "She will do," was his response.

We immediately recognised the magnitude of this break as the show would attract a family audience of over 20 million but we had to convince Pete to get the track finished ASAP to meet the filming deadline which involved Kylie lip-synching to the song while driving around Sydney in a convertible BMW.

With the single finally finished, a release date was set for December 29, and the filming successfully completed with the added bonus that we could use the footage for promotion purposes.

It was difficult to measure the impact of such a major TV show in those days but it was a useful weapon, or so we thought, in convincing Radio 1 to play the record. We were constantly rejected so we reverted to TV opportunities and 'Neighbours' in particular. The BBC press people were very helpful and informed us that Kylie's part in the show was growing and by the end of January she would be its star. This gave us renewed confidence so we kept going and Capital Radio stepped in with DJs Pat Sharp and Mick Brown in particular being supportive. We also had a big break when going live a Saturday morning children's TV show gave us a video showing – producer, Cathy Gilbey totally got it! We were also restricted by the fact that Kylie was not available due to her filming commitments back in Melbourne but Mushroom gave us a break by coming up with a new video clip resulting in more TV coverage.

The single just hovered around in the Top 75 for the first couple of weeks but it was vital to break into the Top 40 in order to secure a Top of the Pops plug, which in those days almost guaranteed a big hit. Most of our team were attending the MIDEM music festival in Cannes at the end of January 1988. We all gathered in the famous Martinez bar on the Saturday night ahead of the Sunday afternoon chart announcement, including key member, Steve Jenkins who ran the independent sales team/strike force Impulse who was confident of creeping just inside the Top 40. On the following afternoon we had arranged for our Sue Foster, back in London, to be tuned in to the Radio 1 Top 40 countdown while I made telephone contact. The entire team, plus friends were all lined up by the pay phone at the Majestic Hotel, all holding their breath as each track was announced. There was nothing but disappointment as our record was not at No 40 or 39 or 38! By then the line up outside the phone booth was rapidly diminishing! Finally, *I Should Be So Lucky* by Kylie Minogue was announced as being a new entry at No 31, way beyond our expectations. Now there was just

Robert Lemon and our friend from NYC, Eddie O'Loughlin with me by the phone but good news travels fast and by the time I hung up and went into the hotel bar, the champagne was already uncorked with Pete holding court – Robert and I searched for a seat! We duly secured a video showing on 'Top of the Pops' and Radio 1 finally came on board.

The single climbed the charts over the next few weeks reaching No 1 where it stayed for five weeks – Kylie was now a star!

With the Stock, Aitken, Waterman now fully engaged and at the height of their powers, a follow up was quickly created in *Got To Be Certain* and set for release in April! This time Kylie was able to come in for promotion appearances and Radio 1 complied with A-list airplay rotation.

We absolutely cleaned up and the single flew to No 2. Naturally an album was recorded which included a remake of 'The Locomotion' which also reached No 2 along with *Je Ne Sais Par Pourquoi* peaking at the same position in October that year.

The 'Kylie' album was released in August and entered the charts at No 1 where it stayed for most of the remainder of the year selling over five million copies worldwide.

Kylie's first album cover – designed by David Howells

Kylie's first album launch with me and DJ Gary Crowley
(then Capital Radio, now BBC Radio London)

To complete an amazing year, there had been a request from the Woolworth chain of stores (at the time they were all powerful in retail records sales) for Kylie to team up with her Neighbours 'friend' Jason Donovan to record a duet, guaranteeing a pre order of 250,000 copies! PWL sales manager and all round, larger than life record man, Tilly Rutherford spearheaded the idea, eventually persuading Pete to make the record. After various ideas being thrown around, the SAW team came up with *Especially For You* which captured the moment perfectly – absolute genius and a sympathetic acoustic guitar solo from Matt Aitken thrown in for good measure.

Unfortunately, Cliff Richard's *Mistletoe and Wine* prevented the record becoming the Christmas No 1 but it did make it to the top for the first chart of the New Year.

We took stock at Sharp End – could we ever repeat such phenomenal success – this had also been the breakthrough year for Jason Donovan and others but those stories are yet to come.

After a short break early in 1989 and after quitting Neighbours, Kylie returned to the PWL studios to record her second album, later to be titled *Enjoy Yourself* and we were all ready for a full on promotion campaign which commenced with a single, *Hand On Your Heart* released in April. We were now in control and were able to choose our priorities in the TV world but we remembered our friends and early supporters such as Cathy Gilbey and her *Going Live*. Moving into a wider audience we booked Des O'Connor *Tonight* which attracted an audience of over 15 million but as the date clashed with the other priority, 'Top of the Pops' we had to plan carefully and gain full cooperation from both shows. The day involved attending TOTP's rehearsals at White City, west London in the morning, driving down to Teddington for a run through with Des O'Connor before returning to west London for TOTPs dress rehearsal and then the actual show recording – we even squeezed in an interview for BBC Children's The Ozone. Finally, we were back to Teddington for Des' show which was recorded in front of a large studio audience – as we walked in to the studios we sensed there was magic in the air, the fans went wild and Kylie's performance of two songs from the new album was stunning. *Hand On Your Heart* entered the UK charts at No 2 going to No 1 the following week. Throughout our time with Kylie, our press officer, Sue had carefully arranged interviews, prioritising pop magazines (our target audience) such as Smash Hits and No 1. PWLs club promotion man, Pitstop also brought in the dance and gay audience – we had just about everything covered. The follow up, *Wouldn't Change A Thing* also performed well and now we had both Capital Radio and Radio 1 onside we were becoming less reliant on TV. A third single, *Never Too Late* was released alongside the album in October which charted at No 1 and sold over a million with 600,000 of those being advance sales! Just for good measure a fourth single, *Tears On My Pillow* was released to extend album sales and also returned Kylie to No 1 in the singles chart!

Another amazing year over – Kylie had also landed her first part in a full length feature movie, *The Delinquents* and was exhausted!

From the beginning we could only admire Kylie's professionalism, work ethic and placid nature which had pulled her through some difficult, at times even insulting interviews. Ahead of her first 'Top of the Pops' performance (the first plugs had all been from video showings), Robert and I attended a dance rehearsal at the cool Pineapple studios in Covent Garden – we were amazed at how well she could dance, absolutely breath-taking. Her manager, Terry Blarney was happy to belatedly tell us that she was a trained dancer – indeed her mother had also been a professional dancer so there was a natural talent in the family. Throughout the first couple of years there was also the underlying issue about her relationship with Jason which we were duty bound to keep under wraps but of course, everyone knew and the *Especially For You* duet made it plainly obvious. Somehow, Kylie had managed to get through literally hundreds of interviews without revealing a thing but overtime this must have taken its toll.

Terry Blarney arranged a meeting with us early in 1990 to inform us that Kylie was 'promo-ed' out and we should go easy on the next campaign. Of course we were sympathetic but we had to consider her forthcoming single, *Better The Devil You Know* due for release in April. By now there were just so many TV shows queuing up to book her, including Pete Waterman's own *Hitman and Her* late night ITV show which was arguably the most exhausting of all. We navigated around this one by stalling Pete until the show came to a London venue (most were in the north of England) and by then Kylie had enjoyed some down time.

However, there were other issues as Kylie was now looking to have more input on her recordings and videos which was against the SAW policy. Terry Blarney's representations to David Howells in the end resulted in him being banned from the PWL offices and studios, so Sharp End were given the added responsibility of being the go-betweens, even when it came to arranging dates for Kylie to perform her vocals.

Kylie was determined to have some control and started making her own videos which were becoming increasingly provocative although the most contentious issue was her desire to work with other writers and producers! There were a few heated exchanges but eventually the compromise was a 50–50 arrangement with Kylie recording six songs in Los Angeles with Michael Jay and Mark Leggett recording *The World Still Turns* with other tracks coming from Stephen Bray who had previously worked with Madonna.

Terry Blarney was keen for Sharp End's support in convincing PWL that these tracks were hit singles but we had to take the honest route – none of them were, and all the big songs came from SAW in *Better The Devil You Know, Step Back In Time, What Do I Have To Do* and *Shocked* – all Top 5 records in the UK. In spite of all the related hit singles, the album failed to reach the level of sales of the first two and peaked at No 9.

1991 was a new challenge in that Matt Aitken had left the team and Kylie's relationship with Pete and David Howells was really tested when it came to making album No 4, *Let's Get To It* which she was contracted to complete. However, common-sense prevailed and Pete stepped up allowing Kylie to co-write with him and Mike and had the brilliant idea of a duet with American soul singer, Keith Washington – *If You Were With Me Now* reached No 4 after the first lift from the album, *The Word Is Out* made a disappointing No 16. An inspired cover of Chairmen of the Board's *Give Me Just A Little More Time*, became the biggest hit from the album at No 2 followed by a slightly disappointing *Finer Feelings* making No 11. Overall a disappointing No 15 peak for the album – this signified the end of an era.

Throughout the year Kylie willingly completed the usual rounds of TV, radio and press and Sharp End's good relationship with her and manager, Terry was still very much in place.

Although PWL released two more singles in 1992 – *Finer Feelings* (No 11) and *Celebration* (No 20) – it was over but with over four million albums sold, would it ever be the same for her!

As Terry Blarney's unofficial advisers, we emphasised the importance of finding a top A & R source – songwriters and producers, as she had enjoyed the cream of the best pop team of the time in SAW who would not be easy to replace. After a year of contemplation, they were seduced by Deconstruction Records, a highly credible dance label which was part of the BMG giant. The label was headed up by Keith Blackhurst and Pete Hadfield who had developed a high reputation in cool house music and they were to be responsible for a ground-breaking album eventually to be title 'Kylie Minogue' her fifth release.

At Kylie and Terry's insistence, Sharp End were built into the deal to continue handling all her radio, TV and press affairs – the first time in six years we had a formal contract with any client. After yet another exhaustive campaign and a big hit in *Confide In Me*, the album fell short of expectations with around 125,000 sales comparing poorly against the millions of her previous releases.

For reasons never explained, Sharp End were let go and promotion and PR moved in-house at BMG – not altogether surprising as it has always been the case that major corporations prefer to use their own in-house staff and this was their opportunity to take it in.

We found some small satisfaction in that there was a break of more than three years before *Impossible Princess* was released while Deconstruction tried to reinvent the Kylie brand, but it sold only half of the previous total – a dismal failure.

We found even more satisfaction when three years on, in the year 2000, Kylie returned to her pop routes and to her rightful place at No 1 with all her subsequent albums and has become a worldwide superstar and a complete legend.

Chapter 8
Jason Donovan

Without doubt one of nicest guys in the business! From day one, he felt like my best friend – full of enthusiasm and positivity. I earlier referred to how his record career nearly stalled before it even started but my guess is that Jason would have made it anyway. However, once on board with PWL and Sharp End, he was like a runaway train, quickly following up his first hit with his duet with Kylie and then another No 1 with *Too Many Broken Hearts*. His debut album, 'Ten Good Reasons' sold over 1.5 million copies and was the biggest seller of 1989 in the UK (following Kylie's similar achievement the previous year).

Jason Donovan with three Sharp Enders and Radio 1 Producer,
Fergus Dudley at his Kensington Roof Garden Album launch party.

Jason was just made for all the available TV and radio opportunities of the time, especially the Radio 1 Roadshow where he even eclipsed Kylie's previous year's attendance record in Newquay where he conducted an interview with Philip Scofield from the cockpit of a Red Arrows jet, part of a display flying over the beach and an audience of more than 10,000. Being such a good sport his popularity at Radio 1 was off the page so maximum airplay was never a problem.

Weston-Super-Mare was another choice location for a roadshow, our thinking being it was the closest to London so could be completed in just a few hours, saving Jason valuable time during his promotion period. On the drive down the M4 from London, I tried to convince Jason that his was one of the more civilised holiday resorts but as we arrived at the promenade there was silence, and then he said, "Do people REALLY come on holiday here?" as we looked on at the weather beaten facades with the clouds closing in.

Jason never complained but his disappointment was obvious thinking how holidays must have been during his childhood surfing the beaches in sunny Sydney and Melbourne.

Another memorable trip took us to Londonderry during the ties of their troubles. We flew to Belfast and had earlier booked a local chauffer services company for a discreet pick up, small car and a coded message to avoid drawing attention. As we walked through the airport, across the PA system there was an announcement to say could "JASON DONOVAN PLEASE REPORT TO EXIT NO 1 WHERE HIS CAR AWAITS!"

The car was the largest limousine I have ever seen. As we made the journey through the war torn streets I noticed we were being followed so I asked the driver if he was aware – "Don't worry, he's with us sir, just in case," was his answer, in case of what I enquired – silence.

We were made extremely welcome and of course Jason's performance was fantastic with another record crowd all going ballistic!

For the return we decided to take the follow up vehicle as it was a modest Ford Siesta, also the limo suffered a strong smell of petrol and seemed somewhat shaky. Radio 1 controller Johnny Beerling partly overheard our conversation and asked if he could take the big car for the return to the airport. Later with Jason having coffee in the departure lounge we realised that Johnny was missing – true enough the car had broken down on route, a close call for us but Johnny did just make the flight home.

As with Kylie, Jason's TV background made it pretty straightforward in securing the best promo slots but there were times when there were just not enough hours in the day to fit them all in. For one (of many) 'Top of the Pops' performances I was volunteered to stand in for him at rehearsals – such a strange feeling being on that stage and there was nothing but sheer relief when I saw Jason walk through the studio door to take my (or his) place.

He almost became a resident guest on ITVs Saturday morning show, Motormouth which was staged live at the TVS studios in Maidstone in Kent. Producer/researcher, Tim Byrne was a huge Jason (and Kylie) fan but he was also perfect for their audience.

Sharp End were also regular visitors to Maidstone, overseeing many of our other artists' appearances on the show – Kylie, Brother Beyond, Sonia, Big Fun, Sinitta, Shakin' Stevens, John Alford, Hazel Dean, 2 Unlimited, Pat and Mick, N Trance, Take That, Boyzone, Sybil to name just a few. Such a strong run gave cause for Tim Byrne to write an unsolicited letter to David Howells singing our praises in glowing terms of how professional we were etc.

Tim Byrne (Motormouth producer) and PWL's David Howells

In 1989, Jason was the biggest pop star in the UK by a mile but remained unchanged and was never phased or affected by the resultant hysteria. These were the days of the mass paparazzi surrounding every event and I remember once arriving with Jason at a celebration being held in his honour at Annabel's in London's Mayfair. The front entrance was just rammed so I jumped out of the car as a diversion with the security team taking Jason around to the back entrance. I fought my way through the mass gathering of media execs and headed for the crowded bar where I bumped into Matt Aitken.

Ever cynical, Matt said, "I don't know what all the fuss is about, he hardly sang a note on the album anyway!"

Of course this was said in jest but there were always a team of session singers in the studio to help out.

'Ten Good Reasons' included two more hit singles in *Every Day (I Love You More)* and *Sealed With A Kiss* and *Especially For You* was added too. Such a huge record, so a real challenge to repeat the achievement. However, once again SAW worked their magic and came up with *Between The Lines* which kicked off with the *When You Came Back To Me* single reaching No 2 over Christmas 1989 only held off the top by the SAW version of Band Aid 2's on which Jason had performed.

The following year met with the album release and three more hit singles with Jason backing up the promo with a live tour, but it was his PAs that made the most impact! Capital DJ, Mick Brown could really wind up audience ahead of Jason visits to the station and there were more Radio 1 Roadshows. TV coverage opened up to include the more adult 'Dame Edna Experience' prime time ITV showed a good 'Aussie' fit.

Throughout our time with Jason there had only been good experiences which also had transferred into positive press coverage, again handled by the Sharp End team. So it was a shock when The Face magazine came up with a strangely negative feature including a reference to him being gay. Jason and his manager, Richard East were mortified and threatened legal action. Our advice was to let the dust settle and we knew there was a more favourable feature to come.

Until this point we were trusted by Richard to handle everything, but with the coming of Jason being offered the star role in *Joseph*, at the iconic London Palladium and more of his old Aussie friends hanging out, we felt things were changing. Finally, Richard decided to teach The Face a lesson and took them to court, Jason won the case but lost in the popularity stakes.

However, he was extremely successful in his stage role and as Polydor had released his version of *Any Dream Will Do*, from the cast album (another No 1 single) – he signed with the major who naturally wanted to handle the promotion/PR in house. His time with PWL was over and a rather disappointing end to Sharp End's involvement, with such a nice guy, we wished him well.

Chapter 9
Pete Waterman

I first met Pete in 1973 when he was in the A & R department of Michael Levy's Magnet Records and he wanted to sign my artist, Nobby Clark, a former Bay City Roller. His enthusiasm was refreshing after the usual cool reception I received from major record companies but it was not a good start when Nobby and I arrived in the Michael Levy's office to sign the contract – unknown to everyone else, Levy had cut the previously agreed royalty rate! We walked out and to my amazement Pete supported our move – we eventually signed with CBS (now Sony). However, I kept in touch with Pete and he regularly came to my Denmark Street office to pick up records to review in his weekly 'dance' column in Record Business Weekly – inevitably we ended up in the nearby shop that sold model railways and he would be buying another Hornby locomotive – I could never imagine that come 15 years later he would be owning the real thing!

Pete was involved in consistent success at Magnet and later with his own company, Loose Ends in partnership with top record producer, Pete Collins who had produced their rockabilly band, Matchbox, regular visitors to the Top 20 in 79/80. However, he really found his place discovering, almost inventing the pop/dance genre after experience gained from his DJ work around the clubs of his native Coventry and the north of England. He was aided and abetted by his local friend and rival, Tilly Rutherford (Coventry's No 1 DJ of the seventies), who was later brought in to PWL as sales and general manager.

By coincidence Cherry Red Records owner, Iain McNay, who became my first client in my own solo venture in 2005, was in the Magnet accounts department during Pete's time there. Later they did a deal for Cherry Red to reissue Kylie's first four albums which I had the honour of promoting again and I was reunited with him after 10 years as we did the rounds.

With Pete Waterman at Radio 2 for the recording of Sara Cox's *Sounds of the '
80s* February 2015

When Pete Collins emigrated to the USA in 1985 becoming the go-to rock producer (Alice Cooper, Rush, Bon Jovi, Gary Moore etc), Waterman set up Pete Waterman Limited with long-time associate, David Howells and discovered Mike Stock and Matt Aitken who changed his life (and mine) forever. Pete had the ears and ideas, Mike and Mike were brilliant songwriters and musicians – this really was THE dream team.

Liverpool band, Dead Or Alive were the first to benefit from the SAW production team with *You Spin Me Round (Like A Record)*, a slow burn but finally reached No 1 in March 1985. Initially they mostly used the Marquee studios facility in Soho but with financial input from David Howells, their own PWL studios in The Borough, south east London, became their permanent base in 1987. Refining their sound and almost inventing HI-NRG in the process, came hits from Divine and Hazell Dean followed by Bananarama, Mel and Kim and

Princess before Robert Lemon and I walked through the door at the time of the Rick Astley explosion and the formation of Sharp End Promotions.

Pete was always keen to give back, even when he had nothing to give other than his talent and his team. Another early hit was in aid of the Zeebrugge ferry tragedy fund, named Ferry Aid featuring Paul McCartney, Boy George and Kate Bush on vocals with guitars coming from Gary Moore, Mark Knopfler and Mark King (Level 42).

During our Sharp End reign, we were happily obliged to work on several further fundraisers starting in 1988 with Capital Radio DJ's Pat Sharp and Mick Brown's *Let's All Chant* for the station's annual Easter *Help A London Child* campaign which rose all the way to No 11. This became something of an annual event and the following year, *I Haven't Stopped Dancing Yet* performed even better making No 9 I Pat and Mick had been huge PWL/Sharp End supporters so it was a real joy to be doing the rounds with these guys, including a few memorable 'Top of the Pops' performances! All in a good cause but just great fun all the way to Bury and back for a 'Hitman and Her' show, co-presented by Mr Waterman himself.

| Pat and Mick's third hit single from 1990. Note the Sharp End sticker R/H corner | With Pat Sharp at the Top of The Pops 50th anniversary book launch, December 2013. DJs Sean Tilley and Adrian Juste to my left. |

Around the same time that year Pete stepped up yet again to aid the Hillsborough football stadium disaster with a remake of *Ferry Cross The Mersey* by Gerry Marsden with other Liverpool artists including The Christians and Holly Johnson – a massive No 1 hit.

Something of a charitable year closed with SAW being appointed by Bob Geldof to remake his *Do They Know It's Christmas* by Band Aid 2 an event which I describe later in my other experiences of working with Sir Bob!

There can be no doubt that Pete changed the face of pop music in the 1980s and 1990s, opening the doors for others including Bros, Yazz, Tiffany, New Kids On The Block, Take That and Boyzone – these last two named were worked by Sharp End early in their careers.

He inspired us all and in particular Mike and Matt until they finally and tragically split up in 1995. At their peak the SAW team could deliver any artist an instant hit and in addition to the PWL roster they gave many others the benefit of their talent including Samantha Fox and Big Fun (both for Jive Records),* Cliff Richard (EMI) and most significantly Donna Summer's *Another Place 8i Time* for Atlantic Records. As always Pete put Sharp End forward to handle the promotion but, just before work started there was a change of heart with the major deciding to do the work in-house – another example of corporate power. This production probably represented the guys at their peak with the Top 3 single, *This Time I Know It's For Real* becoming a genuine pop classic and arguably one of the greatest they have ever written.

It is a conundrum how Pete, with so much success, insisted on invention and reinvention – on one particular Monday morning when inspecting the charts with us, he claimed he had the "Whole Top 10 this week, kid!"

In actual fact he was responsible for SIX of the ten which was unprecedented in itself. There were other much more trivial claims such as winning £5000 at the Ascot races where I was seated next to him – when an assistant came around to take our bets he refused to participate – "Betting is a mugs game kid!"

However, his gamble with PWL certainly did pay off handsomely, never to be repeated to this day.

Chapter 10
2 Unlimited

Something of an enigma – this boy/girl duo became the biggest act to ever emerge from Holland! Their first single, *Get Ready For This* was originally an instrumental produced by Belgian's Jean-Paul De Coster and Phil Wilde and the track quickly became a huge hit in the clubs. Our man with the golden ears, Pete Waterman heard it and picked it up for his newly formed PWL Continental label which meant our company, Sharp End were brought in to handle the UK promotion.

Instrumentals are not the easiest to sell but fortunately Pete flipped the single (in those days we still had A and B sides) which featured some vocals by Ray Slijngaard and Anita Doth who had been brought in by the producers in an attempt to give the track some 'crossover' appeal. Once again UK radio proved unhelpful so initially we pushed the instrumental out as background music (see the Music Week clipping from December 1992) and it was picked up by radio and TV shows which included The London Marathon which brought in massive ratings. Along with all the club action, the track became a motivational anthem for countless sporting events. I clearly remember attending an Ice Hockey game in LA when the track came on at every interval – quite a buzz. Eventually mainstream radio came on board in the form of Radio 1's breakfast show thanks to its producer, Ric Blaxill taking a chance (more on Ric in the Radio and TV Producers chapter) and the single broke into the UK Top 40.

Now things were becoming serious as a 'Top of the Pops' performance was on offer meaning we had to get Ray and Anita TV ready – our team clicked into gear and all went well with the appearance pushing the single all the way to No 2 in the charts with several more territories following suit. Suddenly we had another major act on our hands – coming out of almost nothing.

Nevertheless, Ray was a pretty good rapper and Anita could sing but most significantly they looked fabulous so attracted a massive following from both young girls and boys. Jean-Paul and Phil were providing some great tracks and had a clear idea of the sound required with some executive directions from Pete

Waterman. The records were perfect crossover music, tapping into the rave scene, but also well into the commercial pop market. This winning team went on to produce a long string of worldwide hits – the best known being *No Limit* which hit No 1 in most major markets plus Top 40 in the USA.

It follows that 2 unlimited successes were not without its complications! Ray and Anita were an 'item' and spent all their time together, mainly in studios around the world but also their downtime – this is a dangerous mix and leads to disastrous consequences. There came a point where they would not travel together nor share the same dressing room – Anita was showing signs of depression. To their credit they always delivered on stage but their situation was not helped by the critics – some smart arse DJs quoting, "No, no, no, no, no, no limit: no, no, no, no, no, no <u>talent</u>"; 2 Untalented etc and the UK tabloid press (which Ray and Anita naively didn't understand) were relentless in their questioning about their private lives.

Throughout this time, they hung in there and enjoyed some five years of success, selling millions of singles and albums – always good company even when there was tension in the air.

The producers, who owned the name have made a few attempts to recapture those days in the sun with a little, but insubstantial success – Anita had quit and really was irreplaceable.

The (not so 'difficult') second album –
No 1 in the UK and sold over 3 million worldwide

Get Ready For This, by 2 Unlimited (right) on PWL Continental, represented something of challenge.

However, the company believed that, although they were primarily a rave band, 2 Unlimited had an unusually striking and accessible image and the record had strong crossover potential. Together with Phil France of PWL's own company Black Diamond, Sharp End's Robert Lemon and Ron McCreight

France concentrated on the Mecca/First Leisure DJs bringing in the Manchester based independent club promotion company Reactor to work the rave scene. As PWL was not known for its club music, they worked entirely with white labels and within two weeks of their mail-out, Get Ready For This was riding high in the club charts.

Realising that achieving daytime airplay might be difficult, Sharp End took the

DJs and TV producers stressing its potential exciting background r Capital Radio's Pat Sh started to use it for liu his programme and BBC's Sportsnight also put the track behind action film, particularly football. Other TV programmes including

Chapter 11
Brother Beyond

Nathan Moore/Steve Alexander/Carl Fysh/David White

A boy band with a difference in that they all actually played their instruments, in fact drummer, Steve Alexander was and is an accomplished session man in his own right.

Bizarrely, EMI gained the services of Stock, Aitken, Waterman in a music industry auction at a Nordoff Robbins fund raising event, so they used this 'credit' to progress Brother Beyond's minor success into something much bigger and it worked. My company, Sharp End went with the deal so we promoted the first single under the new arrangement, *The Harder I Try* which went all the way to No 2 in the UK singles chart. Further success followed with the Top 10 single, *He Ain't No Competition* and the related album, 'Get Even' went 'silver' but then their management and EMI decided to focus on the American market.

I distinctly remember attending a meeting with all interested parties (excluding the SAW guys, they had already moved on) at EMI when A & R man, Clive Black stated, "We need to make better records." –

"Better than WHAT?" I asked.

"Well, more credible records then," he replied.

They never troubled the UK charts again and even after a massive campaign by EMI America, only limited success followed there!

It was devastating to watch such a talented band be so mismanaged although I suspected these poor decisions were more to do with EMI than the band's personal managers. On the crest of the pop wave we had created, the band appeared on every TV show in the book including many appearances on 'Top of the Pops'! A highly professional group and always good to hang out with, happily passing many hours of waiting time in between rehearsals and the show (there was a saying among TV pluggers, it is a matter of "wait, wait, wait and wait some more – then rush, rush, rush!").

I remember on one occasion only two of the band could make the usual Friday afternoon rehearsals for ITV's 'Motormouth' as the others were guesting on Radio 1's Roundtable at the same time. So, Robert (Lemon) and I acted as 'stand ins' (Robert on drums, me on keyboards): presenter, Tony Gregory cheekily introduced us as "GRANDFATHER BEYOND"...

It is testament to Brother Beyond's individual talents that they are all still enjoying success in different areas – Carl is a top PR man having worked for Sony and now his own Purple RR company; David has a BA degree in fine arts, showing paintings at exhibitions around the world; Nathan joined successful boy band, Worlds Apart before pursuing a solo career, recently branching out into acting, a really top man; and Steve, continuing with his session work has played for Duran Duran, Jeff Beck and many more. Even original bass player, e.g. White has become an accomplished songwriter winning an Ivor Novello Award for *Leave Right Now* recorded by Will Young with many other successes including Adele.

Chapter 12
Danni Minogue

With older sister, Kylie at her peak in 1990 there was intense competition ahead from 19-year-old Danni as her TV soap, 'Home and Away' ran on ITV against Kylie's 'Neighbours' on the BBC.

They shared the same manager, Terry Blarney who invited Danni to the UK to explore opportunities and she started with an incognito visit to a Kylie live Radio 1 event in Birmingham which is where we first met.

With the audience displaying the usual hysteria, Danni observed the show with curiosity and just a little envy. Terry and (I think) Danni were keen to join the Sharp End roster as it would add weight to her chances of a record deal – Pete Waterman had already passed. We all had a good chat on the train journey back to London although she was not impressed when I returned with a bag full of sandwiches of a meat and fish variety – Danni revealed her strict veganism!

It was not too long before MCA Records singed her and Sharp End were commissioned to set up a comprehensive promotion and press campaign which closely mirrored those of Kylie. We were highly successful with her first single *Love and Kisses* plus follow up *Jump To The Beat* both™ reaching No 8 in the UK, the related album achieving the same number and going gold.

In addition to all the usual TV appearances, Danni was honoured with a Children's Royal Variety Performance invitation at the end of an extremely successful year. Another royal honour came via Radio 1 DJ Peter Powell for Danni to head up various events in aid of the Youth Club ASSOCIATION for which the Queen Mother was patron. The highlight came at her majesty's residence Clarence House where I accompanied Danni in the royal line up – "It must be hard work being on the road," was her comment to me – the Queen Mother's advisers only seem to get a small part of the background.

Not all plain sailing with Ms Minogue – when recording a Christmas special with the ever affable Philip Scofield, there was a 'moment' during a rather complex schedule where Danni acted danced and sang! The floor manager called a lunch break so we adjourned to the canteen where we filled our plates with some fresh salad – then we were suddenly recalled but Danni refused even though there were justifiable reasons. Another time when 'Top of the Pops' reverted to insisting on live vocals, Danni complained about the sound fold back – the sound engineers were extremely helpful and improved the sound, however Danni was not happy and took an early break.

Although Danni's recording career did not reach anything like the heights of her sister, she had a very high profile and following an appearance on Chris Evans' Channel 4 'Big Breakfast' an offer came in for her to stand in for Gaby Roslin as a presenter. Danni's first appearance when plugging her album was in the highly controversial slot, *On The Bed With Paula (Yates)* designed for stars to reveal their most intimate secrets (Kylie has refused the offer on at least two occasions). Danni proved a strong subject for Paula and the interview went well including a great plug for her album.

Kylie watching at home decided she could handle it so asked us to book her in. At the time Paula was married to Bob Geldof who had devised the entire show; meanwhile Kylie was now dating INXS star, Michael Hutchence and Paula took an unhealthy interest in their relationship, a conversation which continued off camera – the presenter displaying an open feeling of envy if not pure jealousy Over time Paula left Bob to take things up with Michael, a relationship which was well documented and which everyone now knows, ended very sadly and badly!

Danni Minogue – a short lived recording career but a highly successful TV celebrity, later teaming up with my old friend Simon Cowell on The X Factor.

Chapter 13
Shakin' Stevens

As we approached the new decade of the 1990s, Sharp End had become the most 'go to' promotion and PR company having established an extraordinary track record over a three-year period – a long time in the pop business.

The offers came thick and fast – one irresistible artist came from my old friend at Epic Records, Andy Stephens (later to become George Michael's manager) in the shape of Shakin Stevens who had already enjoyed sensational success with twenty-five Top 20 singles (including four No Ones) throughout the '80s!

A slight dip in his career had motivated Shakin's manager, Freya Miller to bring in independent promotion and Sharp End was top of the list. Andy was very transparent in that outside assistance would help cool down Freya's aggression and we were expected to manage the manager's expectations.

So Robert and I were sent to the Cambridge Corn Exchange on April 19, 1989, to see his show first hand (I had seen him very early on in his career at the Fulham Greyhound with his band The Sunsets, but that was a very different show)! The sell-out crowd were out of their seats from the first note until the last – people of all ages, all dancing in the aisles and going crazy. We were invited back stage to meet the man – he was charming but somewhat deluded about the current status of his career. When we asked about his availability for interviews in support of the forthcoming single (due May 1989), he referred to his diary and said he was rather busy then – he had written in something which he wasn't sure about – it was in fact the title of his single, *Love Attack* and the release date.

We set to work on the campaign and although Radio 1 airplay proved difficult, we secured an impressive TV campaign which of course included the all-powerful 'Top of the Pops' where his performance was dynamic and very effective. Freya made sure her artist did not move from his dressing room all day, other than for rehearsals and point blank refused permission for him to go to the bar before the show.

Chapter 14
Tom Jones

It was a pleasure to be asked by Steve Jenkins, MD of Jive Records to handle the promotion of Tom Jones's version of the Beatles' *All You Need Is Love* in aid of Esther Rantzen's 'Childline' charity. Sharp End had previously worked on another such fundraising project when PWL released a Sonia (with Big Fun) single, *You've Got A Friend* in 1990.

This time Tom stepped up and agreed to support the release with some radio and TV promotion which actually consisted of a day at a hotel near Sloane Square where a private room was booked for our use. From 10 am until 6 pm, Tom conducted interviews for radio, TV and press with just a 30-minute break for lunch. Just before the final interview he politely asked when we might finish and when we could hit the bar for a nice pint – he certainly deserved it. His other main obligation was an appearance on TV's 'Top of the Pops' which of course was delivered with true professionalism! We had a few pints after the show in the famous TV Centre fourth floor bar in the company of his son and manager, Mark Woodward. Both seemed to enjoy the simple things in life although I'm sure there was much more.

All You Need Is Love for the Childline charity peaked at No 19 in the UK singles chart in January 1993.

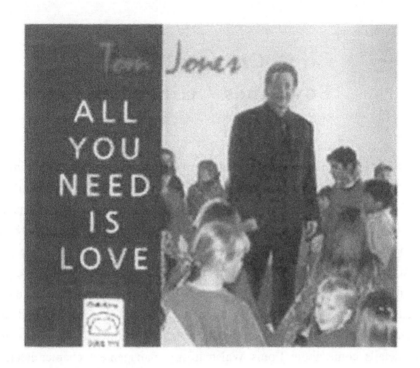

A few years later, Tom was approached by Gut Records' Guy Holmes to record an amazing concept album, later titled 'Reload' which featured duets with Cerys Matthews, Mousse T, the Stereophonies, Van Morrison, Robbie Williams etc. A genius stroke from Guy, or was it his executive producers', Don Reedman's idea? Mid project it blew up, the lawyers were instructed and it nearly went the whole way before a 'courtroom steps' settlement was reached – rumoured to be in the form of one million pounds payment to Reedman. This didn't stop this album becoming the most successful of Tom's entire fifty-year career, selling millions and reaching No 1 in 1999 and again in 2000.

The album spurned several massive hit singles including *Sex Bomb* featuring Mousse T! Ignoring the pending litigation, Tom just kept his head down, did his job and enjoyed a fantastic renaissance of his career. My guess is that his sympathies were with Guy and his Gut label as he simply had to have a working relationship with him to make the most of this unique opportunity.

Apart from various TV performances, I had the opportunity to see Tom in concert at Kenwood House in June 2011 – mutual friend of Guy Holmes, Jon Crawley organised the evening which started well without a cloud in the sky. By the time Tom hit the stage we had torrential rain with little shelter but he sounded so fantastic so we toughed it out – I would not do that for many performers.

Chapter 15
Boy Bands / Girl Bands

In the early 1990s, Sharp End's reputation in the pop world continued to impress and although our latest hit, Damian's *Time Warp* (No 7) was something of a one off, his manager Nigel Martin – Smith was keen to introduce us to his next big thing which came in the form of Take That. We handled their first three releases before they eventually landed their deal with RCA/BMG – the full story comes later when I describe Nigel's management activities more comprehensively, but with the demise of Big Fun, the market was opening up generally for boy, and indeed girl bands. When Robbie Williams went solo, Take That faltered so we stepped up with Boyzone who enjoyed a string of hits throughout 1995 – again more details come about Louis Walsh in my management chapter later. We explored the possibilities in the girl band genre with a six-piece ensemble being developed by Sony but this proved to be a time waster – Simon Fuller then came in with the Spice Girls who he signed to Virgin – they handled their own promotion.

As our press division, now being managed by Liz Watson were representing boyband 911, we once again knocked on Virgin's door pitching to handle their radio and TV, but no joy.

Extremely disappointing and somehow seemed to point to the end of our 10 year run at the very top of the pop business.

911 went on to have an amazing run of 13 straight hits on Virgin, (by now under the EMI umbrella) however, misguided incoming manager, Neil Ferris over spent the budget and the band were dropped – a landmark decision as they had just had their first No 1 single. The word in the business became "pop was too expensive!"

Kylie Minogue	Dannii Minogue
Sonia	Mr Jack Code Red
Euruogroove	N-Trance
Lisa Snowdon	Boyzone
Darren Day	Holly Johnson
Loveland	Stone Roses
Shakin' Stevens	Neil Sedaka
Billy Ocean	Big Fun
Tom Jones	David Hasselhoff
Samantha Fox	Jason Donovan
DJ Jazzy Jeff and the Fresh Prince	Hazell Dean
Clubhouse	Brother Beyond
Pat and Mick	Gary Numan NNuman
Rockmelons	Scooter
Opus III	Sybil
2 Unlimited	Nicki French
Band Aid II	Worlds Apart
John Alford	Technohead
Rolf Harris	Deuce
Tony Di Bart	Diva
The Woolpackers	Phat 'n' Phunky
Milk featuring Dan Falzon Dan Falzon	Richard E Grant
Disco Citizens	Take That

Sharp End's hand out brochure for '"London Music Week'" staged at The Islington Design Centre w/c 25 April 25, 1997, where we seriously participated in the search for new business.

Undeterred Robert and I decided to start SHARP END RECORDS with our own girl band, D2M (Dedicated To Music) who included Mollie Marriott daughter of my hero Steve from The Small Faces and Humble Pie. By now David Howells had left the PWL Empire and managed top producer/songwriter, Steve Mac who was then hugely successful with yet more boy bands, WESTLIFE AND 5IVE – his next work was offered to our new label and given Steve's magic touch we thought we could not go wrong. This time we also were well funded – in a move to get away from their very Irish roots, Ritz Records pitched in along with my old friend Eddie O'Loughlin from NYC.

Alongside a new record company, we also returned to music publishing with funding from Peter Kirsten's Global Music, Germany who had been my sub-publisher for RMO and BRONZE. The best signing to Sharp End Music proved to be Danny Burton, lead singer of The Face, a mod / new Brit Rock band who boasted Ringo Starr's son, Zak Starkey on drums and Gary Nuttall on bass.

I had been introduced to Danny by former Wimbledon football club manager, Terry had originally approached fellow Dons fan, Cherry Red's Iain McNay who had in turn recommended me as his company's business model did not allow for 'development' acts.

The Face were just sensational on the live stage and quickly built a fan base and attracted very favourable press. DJ Steve Lamacq supported them on radio. Danny, a good looking and likable young man, with a strong voice was offered the part of Tommy in Pete Townshend's stage musical but he declined in order to focus on his band. Lady luck dealt her heavy blow when first of all, Zak departed to join The Who, closely followed by Gary Nuttall to join Robbie Williams band.

Meanwhile we heavily invested in the D2M project hoping that the continuing Steve Mac success would spill over but even after some extensive coverage, their two single releases failed and so did we.

Once again we had to refocus our efforts and seek out some new paying customers for our promotion business. With the combined extensive experience of promotion and music publishing we had the idea of offering our services to a major publishing company and pitched the idea to my old friend from Zomba, Ralph Simon who had now become the CEO of Rondor Music. Ralph loved the idea and gave us a lucrative one-year contract and although his stay at Rondor was short lived, his replacement, Richard Thomas was keen to keep the relationship going. The company had a fine catalogue and some fantastic songwriters including Leiber and Stoller, Albert Hammond and by amazing coincidence Steve Mac's songwriter partner, Wayne Hector. More on them later.

When Rondor was eventually sold to Universal in 2000, we really had to find a consistent income stream with ever increasing costs involved in running our West End office.

Following another brainstorming session, probably over a long lunch, we came up with some solid ideas which we hotly pursued.

Bob Grace, an old plugging friend and one-time head of Rondor was running a new publishing company, Windswept Music which had acquired some strong catalogues – set up by Californian music entrepreneur, Evan Meadow and No 1

Japanese publisher Fuji-Pacific Music's Ichiro Asatsuma (another former sub-publisher for my old companies).

After the Rondor experience, Bob wanted us on board!

Robert called upon a golfing buddy, Mario Warner who had just been appointed head of a new Warner Music division, WSM, specialising in TV advertised compilation albums. The result was another nice monthly retainer to work on some classic 'Best of' albums including Dionne Warwick, Aretha Franklin, George Benson, Burt Bacharach, Rod Stewart, The Monkees and Frank Sinatra. It was pretty straightforward as most artists were not available for interviews so we would just pitch for the Radio 2 'gold album of the week' (a Ken Bruce show feature back then) and achieved this with every single one of them. The rest of the campaign simply involved arranging competitions – even the BBC ran them then and Radio 2's Sounds Of The '60s was a good home for those from that decade otherwise it was multiple commercial stations who all had some kind of 'winning weekend' or a weekday equivalent. The exception here was with George Benson who did agree to visit London in support but would only conduct interviews from his Dorchester Hotel suite – a charming man and everyone remarked on his fabulous cologne! The Burt Bacharach story follows.

Next we headed to Sanctuary Records where a former RCA contact, Roger Semon was heading up a similar operation and we hoped the same simple process would apply, as with the Warner releases. They chose to use the 'Ultimate Collection' banner on most albums including The Kinks, Gene Pitney, The Small Faces, Petula Clark, plus various compilations coming from the rich Trojan Records catalogue. However, in many cases Sanctuary's artists were made available for promotion which demanded much more time and effort.

However, the lengthy campaigns that followed with Petula, Ian McLagan/Kenney Jones from the Small Faces and Gene Pitney, were wonderful experiences.

Chapter 16.
Petula Clark

There is no one who has endured for as long as Petula! A child star of the 1940s and still going in 2020, quite remarkable that someone who my parents idolised in their youth arrived on my artist roster come 2002 with Sanctuary Records' 'Ultimate Collection' album.

The album Sharp End extensively promoted in 2002 and reached No 18 in the national album charts – it contained all her big hits including *Downtown*, *Don't Sleep In The Subway*, *This Is My Song*, *I Know A Place*, *My Love* (around 50 in total), as well as some new recordings.

Such a professional, Petula handled the extreme work load of radio and TV appearances with ease and indeed boundless energy. At one point she appeared on so many Radio 2 shows that the station management started asking questions and soon after introduced a system whereby this could never happen again. The campaign ran and ran and the album sold and sold, the perfect scenario (apart from our struggling to get paid by the record company).

During the down time between rehearsals I had many a conversation with Petula as she seemed genuinely interested in other people, including me – we had our love of France in common which helped. At one time I broached the subject of her personal life, starting with her birthplace, Ewell, Surrey as this is where I had lived for a few years. This moved on to her husband, Claude Wolff who in the early days was her publicist. Although Petula avoided getting into too much detail, it became apparent that they were not living together – her main home being in New York City while he resided in Switzerland. Strangely she seemed to feel responsible for keeping Claude in the manner to which he had become accustomed so her work load, constantly touring the world continues to this day.

This thoroughly enjoyable campaign made me realise how much it can be such a two-way thing – Sharp End became popular with the broadcasters all over again as we were delivering such an attractive artist, while the record company were happy with the considerable coverage resulting in high record sales. Thankfully Petula was happy too and it was flattering to think she enjoyed my company – or was she just demonstrating ultimate professionalism?

In many ways, Petula reminded me of a more experienced version of Kylie who herself has now endured the test of time. Both artists have something very special although Petula's success as an actress and genuine,enduring international stardom perhaps gives her the edge.

Chapter 17
Ian McLagan (Small Faces / The Faces)

I was ecstatic when Sanctuary came up with 'The Small Faces Ultimate Collection' and that their keyboard player, Ian McLagan plus drummer, Kenney Jones would be available for promotion. This band had been the coolest thing on the 'Mod' scene in the late '60s and as a teenager during this time, they were a huge influence on my life. They really were my idols!

It seemed totally unreal to actually be working with these guys some 35 years later and they did not disappoint. Ian (Mac) visited London from his home in Austin, Texas and in April 2003, I went to meet him at his hotel, The Sherlock Holmes in Baker Street to discuss the plan. We set of to various radio interviews and met Kenney at the IRN (news) studios in the Grays Inn Road before moving on to BBC Radio 2. They both conducted the interviews with wit and wisdom, but Mac in particular told a great story.

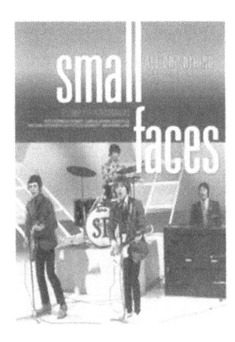

Classic picture of the band, Ian (Mac) McLagan on the right

We quickly struck up a good friendship which resulted in a few more enjoyable campaigns later with his own Bump Band – it became obvious, Mac had to keep working as his ongoing rewards from working with two of the biggest bands of the '60s and '70s (as well as touring as keyboard player with the Rolling Stones), were minimal. The mismanagement of The Small Faces is common knowledge within the music business and even with The Faces, Mac was a very small royalty from record sales – he was rarely credited as a songwriter of any of the big hits even though his contribution was vital. I think I was the more disappointed when his attempt to bring Rod Stewart into a Faces reunion, with just a few (highly paid) gigs, failed. Ironically Rod did finally agree by which time it was too late for Mac, as this reunion was not until 2020 at the Brit Awards!

Considering everything, Mac was remarkably positive, optimistic and had a very forgiving nature, except when it came to The Faces record label, Warners. His opening line in every interview, when asked how he was, would be, "Fantastic, I wake up every morning and play my piano – I finish most days with a live gig in front of wonderful appreciative people."

He was a happy man who had survived much trauma and tragedy in his life which ended prematurely in 2014.

| With Mac at the BBC Radio 2 studios during one of many interviews | Mac with The Bump Band, doing what he loves the most. |

Mac loved his time playing and recording with his own 'Bump Band' which he was happy to share with me by way of album promotion ('Rise and Shine' in 2004 and 'Never Say Never' in 2008) as well as plugging, what proved to be his final UK tour a couple of years before his sad passing.

Such wonderful memories of this warm-hearted, generous, talented man especially watching him doing what he loved best, playing live with highlights being at The Jazz Cafe and right at the end, The Half Moon Putney.

Chapter 18
Leo Sayer

Demon Records released the Leo collection, 'Endless Journey' on November 8, 2004 – Sharp End were commissioned to handle the Radio and TV Promotion.

This was the start of a beautiful friendship with this little man with a big heart and an even bigger voice.

His extensive run of hits began in 1973 with 'The Show Must Go On' and included ten Top 5 singles, two of which made it to No 1 – the latest in 2006, *Thunder In My Heart* (the Meek remix version) which originally peaked at No 22 just 30 years earlier! However, for me his most memorable song has to be *When I Need You* written by Albert Hammond with Carol Bayer Sager (both earlier referred to under 'the songwriters' – Carol was at one time married to the legend, Burt Bacharach). A No 1 record in the UK and the USA and massive on a worldwide basis – a truly stunning performance from Leo!

The story for me really started back in 1981 when I worked at Bronze who had signed Cornish based rock band, The Mechanics (Al Hodge, Dave Quinn and Alan Eden) who didn't really make it in their own right but were so good that Leo asked them to become his permanent backing group – they toured the world extensively for five years and I attended many of these shows which were always spectacular, packed full of hit songs! However, I first saw him live at the MIDEM festival in 1974, hanging out with his famous manager, Adam Faith (also a 1960s' pop star).

Leo centre with The Mechanics' Al Hodge to his right,
David Quinn and Alan Eden to his left.

Leo was a dream when it came to promotion and we booked him on to a considerable number of national shows – TVs included 'Noel's House Party', a high rating Saturday night BBC 1 show. Radio 2 loved him (and still do) so he was special guest on Steve Wright, Simon Mayo, Wogan, Ken Bruce, Johnnie Walker – just about every show really! I particularly remember a live performance on ITV's breakfast show GMTV which required sound checking at 6.30 am! Arriving at the South Bank HQ on time, I was informed that Leo had already arrived so I ran up the stairs to the studio where he was already singing *When I Need You* like an angel (a beautiful song but not easy to sing) – just perfect when it came to tuning even at that *de bonne heurel*. We then had nearly two hours to kill before going live on air, so a long but entertaining breakfast ensued – Leo was just great company.

Although Leo had enjoyed amazing success through the '70s and '80s, it appeared that he had many legal and financial problems, claiming that original manager, Adam Faith had cheated him when it came to fees, royalties etc. As by then Robert (Lemon) and I felt part of his team, we tried various things to help him including finding a good new lawyer and introducing his then manager (and partner), Donatella Piccinetti to all kinds of international contacts at MIDEM.

In the end nothing came of it and Leo emigrated to Australia to a new life although he often visits the UK and it is always a joy to bump into him around the Radio 2 building!

Chapter 19
Eagle Rock / Eagle Vision

One of Sharp End's better moves in the later days was its association with Eagle after a chance meeting with their Marketing Manager, Ian Rowe in our favourite 'corner bar' on La Croisette in Cannes, during one of the many MIDEM festivals.

We had worked with Ian during his time with PWL distributors, Pinnacle and we enjoyed an exceptional relationship – the safest hands in the business with a wealth of experience, especially in the rock genre!

The deal started with a 'one-off' agreement to promote 'The Best Of The Boomtown Rats' album but with an increasing number of music DVD releases coming up, Sharp End were granted a retainer for several years to come.

Eagle would always do things in style and we had the enjoyable task in inviting the media to many prestigious launch events and screenings over the following 15 years. These included Paul McCartney's hosting of the 'Wings Over America' DVD launch at BAFTA in London's Piccadilly (where I was reunited with his brother Mike); Peter Gabriel's 'New Blood' (a 3D DVD/Blu-ray) at Notting hill's Electric Cinema; brunch with Roger Hodgson for Supertramp's 'Breakfast In America'; Cat Stevens' 'Majikat' and INXS's 'Live Baby Live' both at the Soho Hotel.

Perhaps the pick of them all was a boat trip to the 02 arena for Jeff Beck's, 'Rock 'n' Roll Party' DVD launch honouring Les Paul. A star studded group boarded a Thames Clipper at the Embankment Pier only for guest, Ronnie Wood's girlfriend to arrive at the wrong side of the river. At huge expense the boat had to divert to the south side of the Thames to pick her up.

A real coup for the company was in picking up the rights to represent the visual footage from all Montreux Music Festivals covering over 40 years of concerts. Innovator, Claude Knobbs hosted a party at Harrods in Knightsbridge and Sharp End secured a four part series, hosted by Jamie Cullum, for Radio 2.

Eagle also regularly hosted a swish party at MIDEM in their La Croisette apartment suite and one particular year, Justin Hayward played live to introduce the world's media to his solo album, 'Spirits Of The Western Sky'.

Perhaps the most important of all the Eagle DVD releases were the Rolling Stones 'From The Vault' series which covered the band's concerts from the very beginning, right up until the present day. The company's relationship via director, Lindsay Brown with the Stones also led to a solo Ronnie Wood solo album, 'I Feel Like Playing'.

Having established themselves as the market leaders in music DVD, it was inevitable that the time would come to sell the business on… that time came in 2014 at which point Sharp End's retainer was cancelled in favour of continuing on a one-by-one basis. Although Robert and I continued to work together on these projects, which have only recently (2021) dried up, we made the decision to close down our business after 18 amazing years. A timely offer came in from our landlords which paid off some rent arrears and left a small bonus – they were selling on to developers so required 'vacant possession'.

So in the summer of 2005 we closed the doors at Grafton House.

I was lucky enough now to live in Marylebone, just a short walk to the BBC's Broadcasting House and the spare bedroom became the perfect office – rent and rates free! All I needed was some good equipment, some luck, plenty of energy, but there were no staff required.

The end of an era but most definitely the beginning of an exciting new one. Before I start those new stories, here are some about the artists we worked on during our last days as Sharp End, arising from our relationship with Eagle.

Chapter 20
Bob Geldof

I have 'brushed shoulders' with Sir Bob on several occasions – probably the most driven man I ever met and there is no question that he achieved the impossible in staging 'Live Aid' in 1985 raising millions for the desperate people in Africa.

Although I was a peripheral figure at the event, just tagging along with some of the Radio 1 crew (I knew producer Jeff Griffin who handled the sound there), I was very much involved when it came to making the Band Aid 2 single in 1989!

Do They Know It's Christmas was first made in 1984 and featured George Michael, Bono, Boy George, Sting, Simon Le Bon and many more stars – it was written by Bob with Midge Ure and stayed at No 1 for five weeks, selling over two million singles.

A few years later, Bob realised he needed to raise more money for the cause and approached Pete Waterman as the man of the day, to remake the song – this time the artists mainly consisted from the PWL/Sharp End roster: Kylie, Jason, Sonia, Big Fun, SAW + Bros, Cliff Richard, Lisa Stansfield and Wet Wet Wet.

All the Sharp End staff were on board to organise the mass media who attended the recording sessions at the PWL Studios in the Borough, South East London on Sunday, December 3, 1989. The atmosphere was electric with TV and radio crews from all major broadcasters in attendance as well as all major national and music journalists. All the artists were totally cooperative (with the exception of Marti Pellow from WWW) and the resultant coverage was massive – Kylie and Jason were just amazing!

This new version also reached No 1 if just for the three weeks over the Christmas period with sales close to the million mark.

I next met Bob three years later at the launch of Channel 4's Big Breakfast TV show which was originally presented by Chris Evans, Gaby Roslin and 'on the bed with', Paula Yates. Robert (Lemon) and I were regular visitors to the studios at Lockkeepers Cottage in Bow to supervise many of our artists – I refer to the time that Danni Minogue was on the bed with Paula earlier in this book but there were many other memorable moments: a promo campaign for Marky Mark meant a booking on the show, Mark was then a rapper who became, Mark Wahlberg a very successful actor.

In order that he arrive on time, an extraordinarily extravagant plan was made involving Warner Music staff and his personal management and staff. Robert and I were the welcoming party at Bow where he finally arrived five minutes after they came off air. They just couldn't get him out of bed it seems – amazingly the Big Breakfast producers were very forgiving and were willing to re-book him!

It would be 12 years before I met Bob again – this time it was very much full on as it was to promote the 'Best Of The Boomtown Rats' which Eagle Rock were releasing.

We knew it would not be a problem to secure major radio and TV slots but things just had to be planned correctly in order to maximise sales. This was the tough part as Bob, being so hyper just went ballistic when we suggested that we would have to wait to do the Jonathan Ross show as the (Michael) Parkinson how would require an 'exclusive'. However common sense eventually prevailed and we booked him on just about everything over a two month period. The final plug was to be a children's TV show, CDUK hosted by Cat Deeley (originally co-presented with Ant and Dec). Executive producer, Conor McAnally was excited to have Bob on the show as a fellow Irishman, but also because he was independently producing a George Michael documentary and wanted a contribution from Bob once the live CDUK came off air.

On arrival, Conor was all over Bob and hung out in his dressing room, partly to brief him over the videos to be reviewed in their 'hit or miss' item. We all viewed the clips but Bob only liked one of them and wanted to give the viewers the benefit of his (strong) opinion.

"Feel free to express yourself," says Conor.

"Remember this is a children's show," say I.

"No problem!" says Conor.

So, we are live on air, they run the feature but run out of time so only show the two videos that Bob didn't like and when this was announced by Cat, Bob ranted explicitly – the phones light up, Conor is summoned to the office to handle the stream of complaints, Bob is somewhat disgraced but not at all embarrassed.

As we moved back to his dressing room, he said, "Well, Conor won't want me to hang around for the George Michael filming now, will he?"

I advised waiting for things to cool down – quite predictably Conor finally came back saying all was forgiven so it was all systems go for the filming.

When we finally departed the Riverside Studios in Hammersmith, Bob actually thanked me for everything and suddenly seemed incredibly friendly, *why* – he announced he was to do the whole Live Aid thing again, this time in London's Hyde Park to be named Live 8 – he thought I could help. I made a fast exit.

Another massive success, the concert was stage in the summer of 2005 again starring Paul McCartney, Elton John, George Michael and Sting along with some millennials including The Killers, The Stereophonies, the Scissor Sisters, Travis etc etc.

I met Bob again in 2006 outside the Palais de Festival in Cannes where he graciously picked up a MIDEM award with his team, promoter Harvey Goldsmith and IFPI chairman (music lawyer), John Kennedy.

Yet another 11 years passed when I bump into Bob again at a Sky Arts TV show, hosted by record producer, Tony Visconti at London's Union Chapel. Bob performed some Boomtown Rats classics and some Bolan/Bowie – he really delivered. I was fortunate to attend thanks to the wonderful musician who is Nitin Sawhney who had become a friend and was appointed music director for the evening.

Bob could give out grief, insults, praise and sympathy in equal measures but there is no doubt he has a big heart and is truly sincere in his endeavours – probably, above all, he is a rock star carrying with him all the baggage that goes with it.

Chapter 21
Roger Hodgson (Supertramp)

Although I first saw Roger on stage with Supertramp at London's Victoria Palace in 1975, I had to wait 32 years until I finally met him!

The occasion was his arrival in the UK in 2007 for a solo tour and promotion of his 'Take The Long Way Home' DVD, another Eagle Vision release.

We secured a major TV in GMTV (then the top rating ITV breakfast show) when he performed *Give A Little Bit* live, as well as an interview. Radio was covered by Ken Bruce's *Tracks Of My Years* (BBC Radio 2) and Capital Gold's Mike Sweeney show.

I had many points of contact with Supertramp in that one of his original managers was former A and M Records plugger, Dave Margerison, a friend from the BBC promotion circuit and his partner, Kenny Thomson – elder brother of another close friend, singer/songwriter Ali Thomson. Another member of the band (and the family), bass player Dougie Thomson recently (2018) attended Ali's 60th birthday party in the south of France to which I was honoured to be invited!

However, there was deep divide in the ranks by the time I started working with Roger Hodgson, although the dispute seemed to be centred more around the band's other main songwriter, Rick Davies. The legal settlement meant that Roger should bill his tours as "… formerly of Supertramp", whilst Davies could continue to use the band's name.

I had the feeling that Roger carried deep resentment about this but otherwise he proved to be a likeable, charming guy and his live shows were wonderful.

Roger's new management proved to be a curious set up – Lynda Tyler and Shakti who were constantly by his side! So much so that on a second campaign in 2011 (this time to promote his solo 'Classics Live' and another UK tour), I arranged for him to play live on the highly credible Bob Harris Radio 2 Saturday evening show.

As always, Roger arrived promptly along with Lynda and Shakti – we went up to the fifth floor studio to be met by the super friendly and accommodating producer, Mark Simpson and to set up while we waited for Bob to arrive.

A warm, friendly feeling landed when Bob arrived but the two managers had taken up position on the studio floor, one in each corner, seemingly to protect Roger. It was a hard-fast rule that no one should be in the studio except Bob and the artist, but they just wouldn't budge. I offered to remove them but, in the end, both Bob and Mark seemed OK with it and so the show proceeded.

On another occasion (May 25, 2011) following Rodgers live show at the Royal Albert Hall there was an after-show reception arranged in the downstairs bar of the venue. We all arrived in the room about ten minutes after the obligatory encore – several major industry figures in the room (some having travelled thousands of miles), all having a nice chat but where was Roger? We waited and waited – I asked the managers several times when he would meet us? Apparently, he was relaxing and cooling off, but for how long? Finally, as people started to leave, I decided to depart too and, on the way, out passed Roger's dressing room door and noticed it was open. He spotted me and asked where we all were – he had no idea he was being so rigidly protected and seemed disappointed to have missed everyone.

Me with Roger at Radio 2's London studio.

By RON McCREGOR

■ LONDON—Take note all Stateside readers of this column: A&M band Supertramp has something new and exciting to inject into the rock markets around the world. After the impact of their "Crime Of The Century" album they proved their ability to overwhelm audiences with an arresting sense of originality displayed at the Victoria Palace recently. A&M has issued "Dreamer" as a single taken from the lp, and intense airplay should see them into the singles chart following their record success in the album field. A band to watch in 1975.

(remainder of article illegible)

FRANCE

By GILLES PETARD

(article text largely illegible)

RECORD WORLD JANUARY 4, 1975

ENGLAND'S TOP 25

SINGLES

1. LONELY THIS CHRISTMAS MUD/Rak
2. YOU AIN'T SEEN NOTHING YET BACHMAN TURNER OVERDRIVE/Mercury
3. JUKE BOX JIVE RUBETTES/Polydor
4. YOU'RE THE FIRST, THE LAST, MY EVERYTHING BARRY WHITE/20th Century
5. WOMBLING MERRY CHRISTMAS THE WOMBLES/CBS
6. STREETS OF LONDON RALPH McTELL/Reprise
7. MY BOY ELVIS PRESLEY/RCA
8. GET DANCIN' DISCO TEX AND THE SEX-O-LETTES/Chelsea
9. OH YES YOU'RE BEAUTIFUL GARY GLITTER/Bell
10. TELL HIM HELLO/B&B
11. LUCY IN THE SKY WITH DIAMONDS ELTON JOHN/DJM
12. YOU CAN MAKE ME DANCE SING OR ANYTHING FACES/Warner Bros.
13. THE INBETWEENIES THE GOODIES/Bradleys
14. MY FEELINGS (ORANGA) RUPIE EDWARDS/Cactus
15. DOWN DOWN STATUS QUO/Vertigo
16. TELL ME WHY ALVIN STARDUST/Magnet
17. SOUND YOUR FUNKY HORN K.C. AND THE SUNSHINE BAND/Jayboy
18. CHRISTMAS SONG GILBERT O'SULLIVAN/Mam
19. I CAN HELP BILLY SWAN/Monument
20. SHA LA LA AL GREEN/London
21. GONNA MAKE YOU A STAR DAVID ESSEX/CBS
22. UNDER MY THUMB WAYNE GIBSON/Pye
23. HEY MR. CHRISTMAS SHOWADDYWADDY/Bell
24. THE WOMP ROMNY/Rak
25. NEVER CAN SAY GOODBYE GLORIA GAYNOR/MGM

ALBUMS

1. GREATEST HITS ELTON JOHN/DJM
2. DAVID ESSEX/CBS
3. SHEER HEART ATTACK QUEEN/EMI
4. CAN'T GET ENOUGH BARRY WHITE/20th Century
5. ROLLIN' BAY CITY ROLLERS/Bell
6. SLADE IN FLAME SLADE/Polydor
7. TUBULAR BELLS MIKE OLDFIELD/Virgin
8. COUNTRY LIFE ROXY MUSIC/Island
9. THE SINGLES 1969-73 CARPENTERS/A&M
10. SHOWADDYWADDY/Bell
11. BAND ON THE RUN PAUL McCARTNEY AND WINGS/Apple
12. AND I LOVE YOU SO PERRY COMO/RCA
13. THE DARK SIDE OF THE MOON PINK FLOYD/Harvest
14. THIS IS THE MOODY BLUES/Threshold
15. STORMBRINGER DEEP PURPLE/Purple
16. LOVE ME FOR A REASON OSMONDS/MGM
17. THE LAMB LIES DOWN ON BROADWAY GENESIS/Charisma
18. SMILER ROD STEWART/Mercury
19. DAVID LIVE BOWIE/RCA
20. KISS A BOY LEO SAYERS/Chrysalis
21. MOTOWN CHARTBUSTERS VOL. 9 VARIOUS ARTISTS/Tamla/Motown
22. BACK HOME AGAIN JOHN DENVER/RCA
23. MUD ROCK MUD/Rak
24. GREATEST HITS SIMON AND GARFUNKEL/CBS
25. PROPAGANDA SPARKS/Island

My prediction in Record World magazine that Supertramp would be big news after release of their 'Crime Of The Century' album in 1975. The album reached No 4 in the UK and Top 40 in the USA. Best known song was *Dreamer* which was a Top 20 hit single in the UK!

Chapter 22
Ronnie Wood

At first I was quite in awe to meet a Rolling Stone – it was in the Spring of 2010 for a project meeting regarding his 'I Feel Like Playing' album at his manager's office in Wandsworth, just a block away from Eagle's base – they had picked up the rights to release the record.

There was quite a fuss with Ronnie jumping in and out of some press interviews which had previously been arranged by our PR counterpart, Chris Hewlett who was also in attendance along with a team representing Eagle including Robert and myself.

I have always avoided playing the sycophant but this seemed to be expected here as we all tiptoed around what shows would be Ronnie's preference – pretty much everyone would want him on, so there was a choice. However, I played the game for Eagle and we finally agreed on a schedule.

First up was BBC Breakfast TV which was then broadcast from TV Centre in White City but of course it meant a very early start by Ronnie's standards. Something of a military operation resulted in his arrival shortly after eight am – he seemed very proud of himself to have made it (with the aid of 10 people, several espressos and countless cans of Red Bull). To his credit, Ronnie conducted a good interview and the album was given a strong plug on air.

Meanwhile we were back in his dressing room after the show for a chat while waiting for his transport to arrive – Ronnie then had something of a coughing fit, actually no more than just a quick cough or two, but he backed in towards me, hinting that he needed a pat on the back, I ignored this, so his manger stepped in to conduct the procedure; he then turned to me saying "you wouldn't be much good in a crisis," I simply replied, "I didn't realise there was one!"

The worst was yet to come as after a 'business meeting' in The Langham Hotel near the BBC's Broadcasting House, his mood had darkened – the meeting had not gone well. I picked him up in the lobby and with 15 minutes to kill, headed to a nearby coffee house where the manager seemed so star struck he put out a full buffet (rock stars are usually hungry). Rather a waste as we only had time for a quick coffee before heading to the Robert Elms Show studio in Egton House for a live to air interview. Although just a short walk, we were quickly joined by the massed paparazzi – Ronnie was not happy. With just a few minutes to wait, Ronnie declared he needed to go outside for a cigarette, as we were on the second floor, there was no time but he headed for the exit. I ran into the Elms Studio urging them to do something, they put on his album. Ronnie heard it over the PA so turned around enabling me to herd him into the studio and an extensive interview ensued. Another short walk over to BH and Radio 4's 'Front Row' studio followed – poor Ian Rowe and Robert had the unenviable job of holding off the photographers but Ronnie was starting to relax and did a good but long job for the Radio 4 guys. However, we were now running late and were due on Simon Mayo's drive time show live at 6 pm but due to pre-record something for Cerys Matthews at BBC 6 Music. Into the mix came Ronnie's requirements for coffee and a smoke and he disappeared. I went to find Cerys who was happy to reschedule to later in the afternoon – then I had a call from Ian Rowe who had found Ronnie in a nearby Pret a Manger so we just made it on time for the Mayo show at Radio 2. An hour or so later we had finished the interview with Cerys and we put Ronnie in his car and headed to the pub.

A week later we had the Jools Holland's Radio 2 show to record at the iconic BBC Maida Vale Studios. I arrived around 45 minutes ahead of the given time and was pleased to see two guitar 'techs' waiting. They duly set up Ronnie's guitars and amplifiers so all would be ready to go as soon as he arrived. While we waited, Jools, his musicians and I waited in the main studio area next to a long table with several tea and coffee making appliances laid out. Ronnie finally arrived and joined us for a coffee – I pointed him towards the machinery but he appeared puzzled –

"How does that work?" after an embarrassing pause, Jools kindly and to his credit stepped in to make Ronnie's cuppa!

Finally, we were ready to go – Ronnie just had to play one song, an old R and B twelve bar 'standard'. The guitar techs returned Ronnie's guitar, selected one of his diamond-studded straps; Jools counted him in; Ronnie struck up the riff sounding very off – he was playing in the wrong key! Thankfully Jools can handle just about anything with style and grace so the track turned out well and the interview that followed was interesting and entertaining, including several plugs for 'I Feel Like Playing'!

One more TV show to go… 'The One Show' which was being hosted by Chris Evans and (then the newcomer) Alex Jones at BBC White City. Some very difficult planning was involved as the producers had the idea of bringing some of Ronnie's art to display and discuss. There were insurance issues to resolve, not to mention the arrangements for him to get there on time for a live to air appearance. However, all went well and yet another good plug for the album but at the after-show drinks, Ronnie's phone was hot – his Brazilian girlfriend was on her way but lost! He handed the phone to me to guide her in and she finally arrived, by which time Chris Evans had gone home, much to the girlfriend's disappointment. Alex Jones was charming and pacified the girl so Ronnie and Sharp End had a happy ending. After all this effort, the album entered the UK chart at No 164!

Ronnie's own artwork for his solo album released on September 28, 2010

My enduring memory of Ronnie is one of disillusionment, although he seems a better man now, his personality flaws and egotistical indulgence was disappointing, considering he had such a successful and rewarding career. I met him again a couple of years later at his own radio show for Absolute Radio when

I was accompanying Ian McLagan who was plugging his Bump Band album. Mac had played on Ronnie's album – Ronnie had forgotten it all, including my role. Mac had to steer him thought his own show which was full of mistakes and required hours of editing.

Ronnie's guitar skills were hardly a redeeming factor either! – In Keith Richards' book ***('Life') there is a revealing account of how Mick Taylor (a fine player) should be replaced in the Stones – Eric Clapton was considered but significantly, Ronnie had the better haircut and he LOOKED like a Rolling Stone.

(Published 2010 Weidenfeld and Nicolson)

Chapter 23
Justin Hayward (The Moody Blues)

With Justin at the Radio 2 studios for a live interview On Simon Mayo's drive time show, July 26, 2017

Justin Hayward set out to be a songwriter in the late '60s – indeed he was and is an exceptionally gifted composer but he didn't know where his career would take him once he joined the Moody Blues in 1966 – *Days Of Future Passed* was a true classic of its time and started a string of ground breaking albums as well as hit singles including *Nights In White Satin*, *Question* and *Isn't Life Strange*. The band are still touring the world and Justin goes out solo on a regular basis.

I first met Justin at MIDEM 2013 when he played a private acoustic set in an apartment on La Croisette to an audience of international record company execs. This was to launch his new solo album 'Spirits Of The Western Sky'. It was an honour to join him for dinner with his manager, Martin Wyatt and Ian Rowe from Eagle Rock Entertainment.

I set up an extensive promotion campaign for the album – one of the most enjoyable jobs I have ever undertaken – Justin is a true gentleman as well as being hugely talented, modest but justifiably confident with his voice being as strong as ever! I have enjoyed maintaining contact with him thanks to various live CD and DVD releases on Eagle including a live version of that classic album, 'Days Of Futures Passed' in the spring of 2018.

As much as Radio 2 have supported Justin over the years, there was an extraordinary situation that arose in 2017 after I pitched for him to do a live 'acoustic' session for the Ken Bruce Show. The idea was received in a positive manner and a date was agreed. However, the new young producer stepped in to suggest that Justin performed *Go Now* and a contemporary cover (various suggestions were made including something dreadful by the awful James Arthur). Now, anyone who knows their music history also knows that that *Go Now* had nothing to do with Justin – the lead singer at that time (1965) was Denny Laine (who went on to join McCartney in Wings) and indeed the only ongoing members then were Mike Pinder, Graeme Edge and Ray Thomas – Justin and John Lodge joined in 1966. Anyway, the point is that it is an insult to make such suggestions to anyone with such a rich body of work as Justin! However, to his credit, Justin tried to come up with a compromise only to have Radio 2 cancelling the session which was an even bigger insult!

Chapter 24
Procol Harum – Gary Brooker

By the time I had the honour of working with Procol Harum in 2017, it was just Gary Brooker who remained from the original line up from 1967 and anyway, he was always the front man, lead singer, main songwriter etc.

We first met at Jools Holland's studio in Greenwich to pre-record a Radio 2 show for later broadcast.

Later we had a good chat before an interview for the Steve Wright Show – all plugging their new album, 'Novum', their first for 14 years. Gary is a real gent and a total professional – vocally still 100% but somehow his speaking voice sounded a little old and tired. Nevertheless, he gave a really interesting interview.

Shortly after this the band played their 50th Anniversary show at the Royal Festival Hall when tragedy struck with Gary falling from the stage at the interval and breaking his right hand (see picture below). After a short delay, he continued and then after some thought over a few days, decided to continue with the promo campaign too – a true demonstration of the show must go on!

Note that Gary is still playing piano for Robert Elms with BOTH hands.

This campaign was a prime example of the joy of my job. As a kid I wondered at all the 60s' bands including Procol Harum and hugely admired their special talents and now here I am alongside them getting the work done.

By coincidence The PH new keyboard player, Josh Phillips is a sound session player well known to my friend David Mindel and responsible for writing the massive TV series theme to 'Strictly Come Dancing.'

Gary Brooker with me at BBC Radio London for the Robert Elms Show – April 2017,
Note Gary's right arm strapping after falling off stage at his previous gig. Sadly
Gary passed away in 2022

Chapter 25
Independence

Grafton House, 2–3 Golden Square, West Soho – my office for over 22 years

Once the decision had been made, almost for us, to close the Grafton House offices in 2005, there remained only a feeling of great relief and a sense of freedom as never before. The last few years had been a real struggle and for the first time in my career I felt truly independent.

We had enjoyed the benefits of being in a great location – next door housed Virgin Radio from 1993, ten years after we first moved in. The building now contains the Bauer Media Group (Absolute, Kiss, Magic, Planet Rock, Kerrang, Scala Radio etc).

I had already secured a deal with my long-standing friend (and football buddy), Iain MacNay to represent the Cherry Red Records catalogue, and I quickly added a consultancy with Pete McCamley's P & P Songs. So with the continuing relationship I shared with Robert and Eagle, I had three monthly retainers guaranteed, and no overheads to worry about! P & P were a small independent publisher but they represented Burt Bacharach's catalogue and super talented, upcoming songwriter Ina Wroldsen who went on to write over 60 worldwide hits.

Then I set about gaining more new clients and made a big splash at MIDEM 2006 to attract new business. I was delighted but surprised how much work came my way, much of it came from word of mouth. There were some significant events that set me off in the right direction: radio producer, Phil Swern, another long standing friend introduced me to PR man, Dave Clarke of Planet Earth Publicity – I went on to work on numerable projects with Dave, we just clicked as we had the same positive, enthusiastic approach. My other important new contact became Colin Peter who runs an independent record sales and distribution company, Right Track who in turn have a distribution deal with Universal Music.

I first met Colin when working on the Icelandic tenor, Cortes who enjoyed a No 1 album (classical charts) and started a solid relationship which continues to this day.

However, working the Cherry Red releases was my biggest challenge with an ever increasing number of albums coming my way from them, spanning a widespread genre but very little back up in the way of a marketing budget, Iain McNay founded the company in 1978 during the post punk explosion and his big break came in signing American punk rock band, The Dead Kennedys whose 'Fresh Fruit For Rotting Vegetables' made No 2 in the independent album charts in 1980. The company expanded to become the leading re-issues label and during my twelve-year association they increased from around 10 to 50 albums per month! Generally, I really enjoyed this period of my career and loved working with all the young guys in their 'engine room' but found some friction with MD, Adam Velasco especially when they tried to move into the front line of the business with new albums by Pete Molinero and Claudia Brucken. Here are my experiences from just a few of the many Cherry Red artists I worked with from 2005 to 2017:

The Fall

This band defy description and they certainly broke all the rules! Formed in 1976, becoming one of the biggest post-punk bands of the time, probably their strongest releases were on the indie, Beggars Banquet label, they joined Cherry Red in 2011 but a few years earlier they had licenced 'The Marshall Suite' from music publisher, John Fogerty's Minder Music. The new material on 'Sub-

Lingual Tablet' was their best in a decade and one of my greatest achievements for Cherry Red came when BBC 6 Music made it one of their 'ALBUMS OF THE DAY' in May 2015. An EP followed which contained the *Wise Old Man* single and I exceeded my own expectations when I made a successful pitch for the 6 Music playlist. Initially front man, Mark E Smith withheld his permission for the single's release wanting to stay "under the radar"… Who knows why!

The track had over 50 spins on the station over a four-week period. I saw the band play live on one occasion, back *Under The Bridge* but I was underwhelmed – their alternative approach left me cold, I just thought they were a complete shambles. However, my plugging efforts were well rewarded with 6 Music becoming huge supporters and it was touching to hear some wonderful on-air tributes when Mark E Smith sadly passed away in January 2018.

BBC 6 Music's album of the day – a proud achievement for me.

Suzi Quatro

I had briefly met Suzi back in the seventies when her mentor, record producer, Mickie Most brought her in from her home town of Detroit and signed her to his RAK Records. However, he was then stuck for ideas in making records with her. Mickie's brother, my plugging friend, Dave Most asked me to hang out with them just to kill some time and I later discovered that my close friend DJ Duncan Johnson, who was briefly RAK's label manager within EMI, had generously invited her to stay at his house in South West London while she waited. Eventually writing/production team, Nicky Chinn and Mike Chapman came to Mickie's rescue coming up with a very long run of hit singles commencing with *Can The Can* in 1973. Some 38 years later she landed at Cherry Red with her latest offering, *In The Spotlight*, produced by her old friend, Mike Chapman. MD Adam Velasco called a planning meeting with me and various Cherry Red staff, Suzi and her manager/husband Rainer Hass. Suzi had her own occasional series on Radio 2 so there were certainly places to go in terms of radio interviews. However, it became very obvious she was way out of touch wanting to set up a PA tour of record stores – "What record stores, there are none," we all said.

"How do people buy records?" said Suzi.

"Amazon and HMV on line," we replied.

"What's Amazon?" she said.

We moved on to discuss all the TV and radio shows Suzi was convinced would have her on – many of those she mentioned, no longer existed! With her head back in the seventies and being somewhat deluded, Suzi was convinced the album would provide a hit single in 'Whatever Love Is' which was a weak offering and instantly rejected by the Radio 2 playlist committee. The new album was shortly followed by her 50th anniversary box set, 'The Girl From Detroit City' containing all her big hits. I did manage to book some prestigious TV including Channel 5's 'The (Matthew) Wright Stuff' where Suzi's lengthy participation, part of a debate panel, was very impressive. I suppose my problem all along was her music – just never liked any of it and her overconfident, egotistical personality left me cold.

As for MD Adam, I think he was glad when it was all over as part of Suzi's retro thinking was that the record company were there to bank roll her every move including travel and luxury accommodation expenses involved in every interview.

Dodgy

One of Cherry Red's other ventures into the front line business – a new album from 90s' band, Dodgy best known for their Top 5 hit, *Good Enough* and summer anthem, *Staying Out For The Summer*. Led by Nigel Clark and Mathew Priest, the band's main songwriters, they were deadly serious about their comeback album, 'What Are We Fighting For' and I delivered a high level of exposure, most notably on Chris Evans' Radio 2 breakfast show!

Although the related singles failed to make the Radio 2 playlist, there were a number of spot plays and another interview slot on Simon Mayo's drive time. I backed this up with coverage on 6 Music, BBC Radio London, Radio X and Talk Sport but the album did not sell. There were several plotting and planning meetings with the band and various Cherry Red staffers – all very civilised and sensible and I found Nigel and Mathew good company, spending many hours with them at the various radio shows. In the end such an album project requires a good marketing spend along with below the line coverage I could obtain – something Cherry Red have always avoided.

Jack Bruce

Another of my idols from the 1960s when Jack played with Rhythm and Blues bands The Graham Bond Organisation and John Mayall's Blues Breakers, both regulars at my favourite club, The Marquee. However, his best work was of course with Cream for whom he sang and wrote such classics as *I Feel Free*, *Sunshine Of Your Love* and *White Room*. I couldn't believe my luck when Mark Powell, head of a Cherry Red imprint Esoteric, called to say he had licenced Jack's first solo album for 10 years, 'Silver Rails'. I set up some good radio slots starting with Johnnie Walker's Radio 2 show, 'Sounds Of The '70s' and couldn't wait to meet Jack at the Wise Buddah studios, near Broadcasting House, for the recording. I tried to conceal my shock when I first saw him sitting there waiting – liver problems had taken their toll, he had a transplant a year or so earlier. Regardless, he was totally engaging and we had a good chat about the Marquee days whilst waiting for Johnnie to arrive. The Steve Wright show and Robert Elms for BBC Radio London followed – Robert went on to play tracks on a regular basis! However, sales were disappointing as once again there was no marketing budget in place. Just a few months later, Jack sadly passed away on October 25, 2014.

Arthur Brown

In 2016 I was reunited with the intriguing but crazy Arthur after a 50-year interval! I had originally met him in the Noel Gay, Tin Pan Alley offices back in 1966 when he met my boss, Richard Armitage with a view to management. Attempting to describe his stage act proved impossible so he just invited us to see for ourselves as he had a residency at the UFO club in nearby Tottenham Court Road, famous for introducing Pink Floyd to the live stage. I went alone to witness the most amazing show from the 'God of hellfire', who seemingly set fire to his head, well actually his top hat, while performing his million selling single *Fire* and *I Put A Spell On You* – just an awesome show. Although I put in a positive report to the office, they deicide Arthur was not for them.

Oh well, just a million singles later... Now Cherry Red were releasing a two CD set, 'The Crazy World Of Arthur Brown' and although not a priority I wanted to set something up to help and discovered that 6 Music's Tom Robinson was keen. On the day of the interview we both arrived early so there was a chance for a conversation – he seemed to remember or first encounter as if it were just yesterday and we immediately engaged. The interview with Tom ran for an almost documentary-length, as it came to light that Arthur had studied philosophy and law before turning to music so Tom was absolutely fascinated. Arthur is acknowledged by many in his genre as a genius, including Alice Cooper and Kiss!

BBC 6 Music – December 2016
With Arthur Brown at the Tom Robinson Show,

Luke Haines

Almost as crazy as Arthur and certainly as eccentric, I identified Luke as the quintessential Cherry Red artist (along with The Fall) and he was certainly prolific. His band, The Auteurs' 'Now I'm A Cowboy' album, featuring the *Lenny Valentino* single which was held in high esteem in the indie sector in the mid '90s but moving into a solo career in the millennium years, a whole string of releases emerged! I worked on five albums over a three period starting with 'Rock and Roll Animals' in 2013, shortly followed by 'New York in the seventies', 'Adventures In Dementia', 'British Nuclear Bunkers' and 'Smash The System'.

In spite of his unorthodox behaviour, I could feel a good heart beating inside and it was always a joy to be in his company. Luke's live shows were something to relish, pure but demented entertainment but his radio coverage was limited to 6 Music and then mainly Gideon Coe's late night show.

The House of Love

This band from south London, formed by guitarist Guy Chadwick and who became part of the Creation Records' Brit Pop phenomenon of the mid '80s. Something of a comeback album, 'She Paints Words In Red' was released by Cherry Red in November 2013 but compared poorly with their earlier, 'House Of Love' top ten albums and successful singles, *Christine* and *Shine On*. I uncovered some fans at 6 Music, especially producer Adam Hudson, so gained some support there with the band performing a session for the station. Otherwise, the feedback was not good, so in an attempt to rouse more interest I took along some producers to see the band's live show at Scala in Kings Cross, London. The beginning of the show was a total shambles and quite embarrassing as front man, Guy's amp blew up and a roadie tripped over some cables cutting the sound. Several minutes passed before normal service was resumed but thankfully most of the producers attending were such big fans, all was forgiven – not by me though. Later Cherry Red released a 30th anniversary box set of their earlier recordings and a short tour was arranged to support the release – I managed to miss those shows but just hope they had put in some rehearsal time by then.

Toyah Willcox

One of my very first Cherry Red projects was to promote Toyah's 'Safari Records Hits Collections' in 2005. She certainly had some hits; *It's A Mystery, I Want To Be Free, Thunder In The Mountains* and *Brave New World* all struck gold on the back-of-the-punk meets new-wave trend with a Madonna-esque touch. I was not totally, but just a little surprised how the media reacted in such a positive manner and I quickly had Toyah booked on several high profile shows including Jonathan Ross. She was very candid in her interviews as well as being truly interesting and entertaining – a total professional. Even chairman, Ian McNay commented on her raised profile, a rare but welcome compliment indeed.

Jah Wobble

In order to avoid incrimination, I will avoid saying too much about this dreadful and, in my view untalented man! His drug fuelled efforts with PiL left me cold as did his comeback album, 'Yin and Yang'. Cherry Red's John Reid had high expectations so I adopted my usual professional approach and went plugging but the feedback was as expected with the exception of some Gideon Coe airplay and another 6 Music presenter, the dedicated Chris Hawkins requesting an interview. Having made all the arrangements with John for a pre-record in London's Western (now Wogan) House, I waited with Chris and his producer in reception – the agreed time came and went so I called John who reported back that Mr Wobble was not far away. As I sat holding his security pass, he finally stormed through the front door, ignoring us all and going straight to the reception desk – the attendant nodded towards us, I stepped up and introduced him to Chris and his producer but he was obviously not talking to me.

As we went through to the studio he turned to me and said, "Are you still here?"

In an attempt to cover the embarrassment, Chris found himself apologising to me but I just left them to it. I later discovered that Mr Wobble was upset with me as he held me responsible for the album's dismal performance which he found hard to take as it was his first after recovering from his drug and alcohol addiction. Sorry, just unacceptable behaviour, so no sympathy from me.

Pete Molinari

I was surprised that Pete's American manager, Gary Stamler (who had previously represented top Australian band, Crowded House) had persuaded Adam Velasco to pick up Pete's 'Theosophy' album! Although he had some good credentials having appeared on the much coveted, 'Later With Jools' TV show, he was relatively unknown so this was a 'risk' signing. The writing was on the wall when Adam asked me to meet manager Gary on his arrival in London to soak up the early pressure – having plenty of experience, he was no pushover but we had an enjoyable dinner and went through the plans for the album launch. Gary had secured Upstairs at Ronnie's (Scotts) club for an album reception and reluctantly Adam had agreed to put a modest £200 behind the bar. After some hard work I had secured an impressive guest list but this meant the drinks allocation would be rapidly taken up. After some persuasion, Adam upped the limit to £300 but I still had to buy some latecomers a drink. As an incentive to get the media to attend, I had offered them dinner at the trendy Little Italy restaurant right opposite Ronnie's. Although only around five guests took up my offer, the bill was still well over £300! The album did OK and Pete proved popular with several radio DJs, particularly Gideon Coe and Radio London's Gary Crowley – I kept things rolling for as long as possible as I also found Pete genial company but finally it became another example of Cherry Red's underestimation of the front line business.

The worst was yet to come.

Claudia Brucken

My previous experience with producer, John Williams had been with Petula Clark as he had produced a few tracks with her and he had become our 'point' man at her record company, Sanctuary. Over the years I had always found John's attitude to fluctuate depending on who he was talking too – a tricky customer. Now he had convinced Adam to sign a solo deal for Claudia Brucken, formerly vocalist with synth-pop band, Propaganda who had minor success with their 'A Secret Wish' album in the mid-80s. Although the band were held in high esteem by the press and being part of Trevor Horn's stable, ZTT gave them some short lived credibility, I could not see the attraction. Now, some 30 years later, with a new album complete, John cleverly invited all interested parties to his back garden studios for a playback session which was also attended by Claudia herself. He made us very welcome and laid on a spread of food and drinks before we listened to the entire album – I withheld my considered opinion – just a weak selection of songs and below standard vocal performance. Although the Cherry Red guys seemed to like what they heard, no one can give their honest opinion given these circumstances. *Where Else* was subsequently released in October 2014 and I again adopted a professional approach in searching out support. I did unearth some old Propaganda fans at Radio 2 and arranged a live session for Paul Sexton's show when he was sitting in for Bob Harris, an interview with Janice Long and Sara Cox! I rounded up an impressive group to attend her St Pancras Church gig including some 6 Music producers which resulted in a few spins there. Thinking enough was enough, I went on holiday but Williams wanted more trying to squeeze more life out of something of a dead horse from day one.

Playing the politics, he then complained to Adam about my absence – it didn't end well.

With the CD market shrinking and having trained up Cherry Red's in house PR to do some radio, Adam decided I was surplus to requirement after 12 highly rewarding years.

Although the Cherry Red work was pretty much a full time commitment, it was not enough to fulfil my financial needs so I jumped at the chance of working with Colin Peter's Right Track, initially on Icelandic tenor, Cortes taking me out of my comfort zone into the classical world! Although this proved to be an enjoyable and successful campaign, there was much more to come.

Next up was singer-songwriter, Lisbee Stainton who was originally recommended by music publisher friend, Stuart Hornall. Her album, 'Girl On An Unmade Bed' spawned three Radio 2 playlist singles starting with *Red* which strangely enough, 6 Music presenter, Tom Robinson initially championed. In the preceding period, Lisbee's father and manager, Clive Stainton invited me to see her perform as part of a scout/guides jamboree at the 02 Arena. Although most of her performance was part of an ensemble, amazingly she had her own short set – sitting on her own right there in the centre of the stage in front of 20,000 fans, singing her own song, the magical *Red*. Although her distribution moved to Nigel Reveller's Active Media, I worked on Lisbee's three following albums and she toured the world supporting Joan Armatrading. The highlight for me was to see her play a full set at the Royal Albert Hall! Although she never set the charts on fire, Lisbee sold thousands of albums and has enjoyed a fulfilling career – I was proud to have been a part of it.

In some ways this became the blueprint for many of the artists I have worked with during this period – with record sales in decline and the live market opening up, there has become an entirely new way of defining success. Indeed, Dave Clarke's career moved almost completely towards promoting live shows with considerable success with the likes of the 'Strictly Come Dancing' stage shows!

Following these lines, I staged countless showcases for many new artists at the BBC Club – a venue that virtually guaranteed a healthy turn out. Lisbee benefitted with one of these shows early on, followed by Joe Cang, soul/jazz singer and songwriter who was one-time bass player with Scritti Politti and wrote a big hit for Aswad in *Shine*. Following a BBC Club performance his single, *Make Love* made the prestigious Radio 2 playlist which opened many doors for him. I have probably seen him play live more than any other artist in my entire career, most recently as part of Loco Ironico with Italian virtuoso, Matteo Saggese. I was lucky that both these talented guys have become close friends!

L–R: Joe Cang / Matteo Saggese at Pete Gordeno's wedding – Pete is another hugely gifted musician/songwriter and although a good friend, I have not yet had the opportunity to work with him – often he is extremely busy touring with Depeche Mode.

The BBC Club proved to be a very valuable asset over many years – there is quite a list which includes one of the most successful songwriters the UK has produced, Graham Gouldman (I have covered my full involvement with him earlier) who drew a record attendance; The Dunwells who came a close second and scored a record deal with Universal who took it all over and then they disappeared without trace; Mim Grey a highly acclaimed session singer (Paul McCartney, Tom Jones etc) who stepped into the spotlight to achieve Radio 2 playlist success; American Idol winner, Katrina who was produced by Vai Garay (known for his work with James Taylor, Linda Ronstadt and Bonnie Raitt); Mauro Dirago who I original met when he was on the PWL roster but went on to work on some amazing projects including one with Pricilla Presley – *If I Could Dream*, an Elvis No 1 album with the RPO.

Unfortunately the club was forced to stop these live shows in 2014 due to local residents' complaints about the noise levels and it then closed for refurbishment. During this period I was forced to use the 229 venue just up the road in Great Portland Street and the St James Theatre in Victoria – neither venue had the same advantages and I was delighted when the club reintroduced live 'sessions' albeit on an acoustic stage. First in was the super impressive Nashville artist, Megan Linsey who lifted the roof with her powerful vocals. I enjoyed some coverage on her single, *Freak For The Beat* but otherwise the results were disappointing considering her incredible talent – sadly the BBC had started to close its doors to this genre of music.

Megan Linsey on stage at the BBC Club in October 2017

With Mauro Dirago in the Abbey Road Studios mastering suite for his own 'Rewind' album which featured collaborations with Boy George/Rob Davis, Kate Robbins, Julian Smith (saxophone) and Marco Mastrocola (all other instruments), pictured on the left.

My history of success with singer-songwriters resulted in, George Martin's son, Giles offering up a brilliant talent in Dan Clews via his manager, Patrick Cousins (partner in Cousins-Brett music industry accountants). Dan was like an early version of Ed Sheeran – irresistibly engaging on the live stage and a promising songwriter. His *Saltry Man* was added to the Radio 2 playlist in 2009 and was distributed by Right Track. Dan had an engaging stage presence and dialogue which included the story of how he ran over his car over his acoustic guitar, constantly self-repairing it, but this made the instrument difficult to tune – I eventually convinced him that he should at least have a spare. Giles Martin was very supportive and came along to one of Dan's shows at 'The Social' in Little Newport Street, in the west end of London. We had a good chat and he agreed to guest on Bob Harris's Radio 2 show with Dan, accompanying him on keyboards for a live session. Giles also joined in the interview with some fascinating Beatle stories – he went on to mix the multimillion selling 'Love' album, soundtrack to the Cirque de Soleil's sensational Las Vegas show.

I have written earlier about the tremendous worldwide success of songwriter Jamie Hartman and I was privileged to promote some his early efforts which he released under the Ben's Brother pseudonym enjoying Radio 2 playlist success with *Let Me Out* and *Stuttering* – his 'Beta Man Fairy tales' album charted at No 14 in the UK! There were several memorable live performances too but really the Ben's Brother work was the precursor for Jamie as a top songwriter for other artists, over many years.

Other 'new' singer-songwriters on my roster were Allie Moss from New Jersey whose song *Corner* was used as a BT Infinity TV commercial and charted in the UK. This time I had the opportunity of utilising the BT Tower for the launch party – plenty of food and drinks to accompany the music as the tower rotated; Jeff Lowe, well known for his superb guitar playing on the session and live circuit, developed a consortium named GEM (Groove Enlightened Minstrels) and made some fascinating albums which unfortunately proved to be too sophisticated for their natural home Radio 2.

My friend since 1972, David Mindel came up with an interesting new album, 'Issues' by a Band Of Sisters, a cooperative of some of the best UK female vocalists including PP (Pat) Arnold, Tessa Niles, Miriam Stockley, Stevie Lange and Mandy Bell (also Mim Grey with whom I worked on her solo efforts).

The first single, again released by Right Track, was Pat's *Gratitude* and she was a delight to accompany on the promotion trail. PP Arnold was a 60s' soul great and enjoyed hits with *The First Cut Is The Deepest* and *Angel Of The Morning* but was just sensational guesting on the Small Faces' immense single, *Tin Soldier*!

Although he has lived in the south of France for many years, the music has never left him – in particular the Eurovision Song Contest has never left him! I worked with him on his attempts in the seventies with Olivia Newton John and The Shadows (he had a few more too), then all these years later in 2016 he wrote (with Adrian Bax-White, another ex-pat) Electro Velvet's *Still In Love With You* which became the UK's entry that year. Of course it finished 24th as is the norm for us these days!

No matter what format the BBC devise for the UK entry, we inevitably finish in the bottom five.

Nevertheless, we had much fun with the promotion with Radio 2 getting behind it including a live session for the Graham Norton Saturday morning show.

David Mindel and veteran Norwegian music publisher, Philip Kruse on my left, at one of our celebrated Midem/Cannes beach lunches. Philip represented David's Eurovision songs for the Scandinavian territories during the seventies.

During this period I was also lucky enough to be offered projects involving some true living legends – in particular I enjoyed the Graham Gouldman campaigns and there was a short lived run with Gilbert O'Sullivan via Union Square Records in 2012. Then there was Jim Lea, Slade's bass player and co songwriter with Noddy Holder – a lovely talented man but he was restricted with performing at this time due to health issues.

I had known Roy Orbison's wife, Barbara from our time as consultants to Rondor Music and I ran several campaigns with her preserving the 'Big O' legacy including a three-part series for Radio 2. We exhausted every promotional opportunity along the lines of the anniversary of his passing, his birthday and other landmarks until her own untimely death in December 2011.

More recently I worked on the multi-talented, Barry Adamson album, 'Know Where To Run' – what amazing energy with his film making, composing, photography and musicianship. No shortage of interview material and BBC 6 Music were particularly supportive. Another brilliant live performer too.

Popular musician, Phil Pickett asked me to promote his autobiography, 'Calmer Chameleon' – many stories about many artists, particularly Boy George and Culture Club as Phil co-wrote the hits, *Kama Chameleon* and *It's A Miracle*. I certainly enjoyed this adventure, and later I did some work for a new band he managed with his son Harry, Shake, Shake Go who made it big in France (the band were French except for singer Poppy who is Welsh). I arranged another BBC Club launch party which went pretty well but they never repeated their French success in the UK.

Phil Pickett in the 70s

The joy at this stage of my career was how I was drawn into such a wide variety, outside of my usual comfortable zone of pop, rock and soul:

Reggae, in the form of ex Aswad front man, Brinsley Forde with whom I scored two Radio 2 playlists before he lost his way again; I tried to leave this genre alone from then on, except Right Track offered up an album by Osibisa (another blast from the past courtesy Bronze Records), their first for 20 years but theirs is best described as African/Caribbean music.

Folk, with the charming Moya Brennan – during her album campaign, I accompanied her to the Radio 2 Folk Awards and Maev who was part of the Celtic Woman ensemble. I hosted a BBC Club showcase for her which resulted in a slot on the highly rated Radio 2 'Friday Night Is Music Night' in 2013.

Urban – legendary publisher, Lance Freed appointed me as UK representative for LA based urban singer, Goapele with the big challenge of arranging a special night at the Jazz Cafe as part of her UK promo trip. I hired the venue and identified the upstairs bar as the perfect VIP area which much to my relief was fully supported by the media. The club manager suggested also selling tickets and the 'walk up' business resulted in enough money to cover the entire costs of the event – Lance was delighted but the Universal Music accounting system found it difficult to handle 'refunds'! I really rated Goapele but generally this genre leaves me cold so avoided getting involved beyond this.

Jazz – Cherry Red released the James Taylor Quartet's 'Rochester Mass' album in December 2015 and Dave Clarke effectively handled the press promotion. The work of a genius musician but rather ambitious for the CR team. I did witness a magnificent performance of the work at the Ronnie Scott's Soho jazz club but sales were disappointing. Right Track released Pete Long's 'Planets' concept album and the promo campaign was reasonably successful with several radio interviews including Jools Holland for Radio 2 and Robert Elms on BBC London. Pete, another Ronnie Scott's regular along with legendary session man, Mo Foster whose 'In Concert' jazz album I promoted for Right Track in 2021. A more traditional outfit were the Jive Aces – a highly entertaining live jive act but proved to be a tough one for radio – Jo Good on BBC Radio London was hugely supportive and I came close on some major TV – they were semi-finalists on Britain's Got Talent in 2012. Trombonist Aubrey Logan was and is a delight, a unique talent and I was pleased to run the campaign for her debut album, 'Impossible' in 2017. My major break with her was (yet again) the Jools Holland Radio 2 show and this opened the door for her UK tour(s) – she also played at the highly prestigious Montreux Jazz Festival.

Jazz Festival; Aubrey Logan recording her session for the Jools Holland show.

Classical – slightly out of my depth but I managed to develop a close relationship with the Classic FM radio station in the form of managing editor, Sam Jackson and head of music Phil Noyce. These true gentlemen were a joy to deal with and would listen carefully to what you had to say over a nice cup of tea, very civilised! First up in 2007 was Icelandic tenor, Cortes which came to me from Right Track and resulted in a No 1 album in the classic charts. Then came clarinettist, Lone Madson and her 'White Sands' album which enjoyed brief success in 2009. A few years later, in 2014 came Rhydian. A Welsh tenor whose 'One Day Like This' album was released on agent, Neil O'Brien's Futura label. Again Classic FM were helpful and I arranged a major interview with Justine Greene who had a high rating Sunday afternoon show ahead of the chart rundown. Justine was magnificent, Rhydian was reluctant and disliked the choice of tracks they played – he openly criticised his own recordings, bizarre! He proved to be a very tricky customer and sadly this affected my previously good relationship with Neil. Italian cross over trio Il Volo sold out the London Palladium and the Royal Albert Hall but were so busy with worldwide tours they never took up Classic FM's offer of a live session, again rather bizarre. Finally,

I worked on the charming female soloist, Justine Balmer – Phil Noyce attended her live shows and he offered comprehensive advice about the way her album should be recorded if targeted at a Classic FM audience. Her management delayed as they sought funding or a major record deal so most of the momentum was lost although her *Simple Thing* was finally released by Right Track in July 2019 and indeed received airplay on the station.

Sarah Class has a reputation in composing for TV and film but she made a brilliant vocal album, 'Unity' in 2015 so Dave Clarke and myself teamed up on the promotion and PR. The album was classified as 'crossover/classical' but my contacts at Classic FM could not find anything that suited their programming. In the end it was Radio 2 who came on board with plays on the single, the title track and Good Morning Sunday booked her for a live session. At this time the BBC Club was closed for refurbishment so I arranged a showcase at the St James Theatre in November 2015. Although well-attended, including senior record company executive, David Munns (being a long standing mutual friend), the show was not a huge success with Sarah seemingly nervous and out of her comfort zone. However, later in the campaign Sarah's association with Sir Richard Attenborough, from her music for several of his TV series (including the BBC's six part 'Africa') gave her the opportunity of Sir Richard featuring in her video for *I Will Fight* the lyric giving out a highly personal message about this beautifully on Radio 2's 'Good Morning Sunday'!

Sarah Class with the legendary Sir Richard Attenborough

With Dave Clarke and David Munns at the St James Theatre.

Indie – Cherry Red was founded in the post punk era so had a foundation of so called 'indie' bands such as The Fall, The Dead Kennedys, the Mo-dettes, The Membranes, House Of Love, Felt, Luke Haines, Jim Bob, the Monochrome Set. All these bands had an energy and an attitude representing a new spirit being the perfect antithesis to the super smooth 'public school' groups that had previously dominated – Genesis, King Crimson, Yes, Roxy Music, etc all very musically talented but considered by the new generation to be rather bland. However, I have to agree with George Martin (*All You Need Is Ears* (p)1979 St Martin's Griffin) when describing Bach as the pop/rock musician of his day, saying that "the one thing he wouldn't have been doing is punk rock because he was musical and punk rock wasn't – it was a separate phenomenon altogether!"

I enjoyed working on these artists' mainly re-issued albums, but seeing them live was sometimes an embarrassment as many displayed very limited musical ability. However, I was also delighted to be part of Cherry Red's expansion into the mainstream market and they now have an impressive catalogue (albeit mainly on a non-exclusive licence basis) including some of the all-time greats: lOcc, The Blow Monkeys, Dr John, Miles Davis, Michel Legrand, John Barry, The Move, Doris Day, Dusty Springfield and Jack Bruce, releases that will tell you how wide and varied their list has become.

Dr Robert leading the Blow Monkeys at live session for Vintage TV in November 2017.
One of Cherry Red's better "signings"!

Blues – one of my biggest influences from the Chuck Berry days and the Rolling Stones + my own little 'beat' group covering Chuck as well as John Lee Hooker, Willie Dixon, Muddy Walters etc. In 2011 Albany Down arrived on my desk from my clients Arising Artists – an extremely accomplished blues band managed by guitarist, Paul's father Dave Turley. I arranged yet another BBC Club showcase on March 24, which resulted in a live session for Radio 2's Blues show presented by legend, Paul Jones and further national radio support came from Alex Lester and Janice Long. The band continue to do well on the live circuit to this day.

ALBANY DOWN at the BBC Club with Paul Jones' Radio 2 producer, Paul Long on my left.

Rebecca Downes is an award winning blues soloist and I was honoured to represent her radio media interests during 2017. The previous year, Rebecca won Best Female Vocalist and Best Emerging Artist at the British Blues Awards and a year later in 2018 she won the British Blues Federation's Female Vocalist of the Year award. Rebecca's 'Believe' album was produced by Chris Kimsey, best known for his work with the Rolling Stones, Pete Frampton and Joan Jett – it included the *Sailing On A Pool Of Tears* single which Radio 2 included on their Paul Jones and Alex Lester shows and Robert Elms booked her for a live session. Otherwise Rebecca really is at her best on the live stage – she played a memorable gig at the St James Theatre in London's Victoria to a full house. I'm happy to say that she is still on the road doing what she loves.

In 2007 I also enjoyed a brief period working on award winning blues favourites, Deborah Bonham, Matt Schofield and Ian Siegal but opportunities at radio were limited to Paul Jones' blues show and Jools Holland. Both are tremendous performers on the live stage and I was lucky to attend a special blues extravaganza at Harrods department store in Knightsbridge. Both artists continue to play to full houses at all the blues venues around the UK including the Jazz Cafe and the Bulls Head in London.

Chapter 26
Allan Clarke (The Hollies)

I previously described how I first met Allan when my artist, Gary Benson became special guest on a Hollies European tour in 1975 and how Gary went on to co-write for one of Allan's solo albums. I completed the full circle when I met up with Allan again, initially when he supported the Hollies' documentary DVD, 'Look Through Any Window' for Eagle and again for his 'Sideshow Solo Recordings' three CD release for Cherry Red. Along with The Beatles and The Stones, The Hollies had the most impressive number of hit singles in the '60s, continuing into the '70s – I bought every one of them.

All these years later, it was a pleasure to meet up with him again, a lovely man but he cut a somewhat sad figure having suffered personal problems and his enforced retirement from performing as his, once most powerful voice, had suffered. Happily, he did make a comeback performing with his friend Graham Nash at their induction into the Rock and Roll Hall of Fame in 2010. I have also heard recently that there could be a comeback Hollies tour in 2022, I will be first in line if it happens.

With Allan Clarke at the Robert Elms Show, 2011

Chapter 27
The Blow Monkeys

October 4, 2017 – Dr Robert (Howard) at Robert Elms BBC Radio London studio.

I first met Dr Robert in 2012 when Cherry Red Records re-issued the Blow Monkeys' albums, first released in the '80s – 'Animal Magic', and 'She Was Only A Grocers Daughter' – the latter including the brilliant classic hit, *It Doesn't Have To Be This Way*! Robert has a voice full of soul and is a great guy all round. A more comprehensive campaign with Cherry Red started in 2013 for a new album, 'Feels Like A New Morning'. The band played London's Bush Hall as part of the promotion – they were absolutely sensational, even after all these years.

Things went quiet for a while and then Robert approached me independently with a new album – 'The Wild River'. The first single from the album, *Crying For The Moon* achieved massive airplay on BBC Radio London but strangely was overlooked by Radio 2. With some creative input from the legendary record man, Dick Leahy, a rework is underway as we speak, or rather, as I write and this song has the potential of being a real soul classic!

I should say that, apart from being a close neighbour of Dr Robert in Spain, Dick Leahy was long-time associate and music publisher for the other legend that is George Michael – Dick also had the positions of Managing Director of Bell Records (David Cassidy, Dawn, Showaddywaddy etc) and GTO Records (Donna Summer, Billy Ocean, Heatwave, Fox, Dana, etc). Dick was a truly 'hands on' and remarkably successful exec and directly influenced a multitude of British talent.

Back with Robert, we spent most of our time talking football – he is a massive Chelsea FC supporter whose dreams came true when playing the relatively new venue at the famous Stamford Bridge stadium, *Under The Bridge*. He was also asked to contribute to the Chelsea FC in house magazine which I think he considered one of his greatest honours!

Chapter 28.
Christopher Cross

On Thursday, December 3, 2009, I am at St Pancras station, London, waiting for the Eurostar train from Paris – it's winter, the train is late but I have to get Christopher Cross to BBC Radio 2 by noon to record the Ken Bruce Show's 'Tracks Of My Years' feature!

His record company representative, John Waller is waiting with me but not helping! No transport has been arranged to move us from the train station to the radio station and the queue for cabs is horrendous – this is happening in pre-Uber times.

I finally track down the revised arrival time so position Mr Waller at the platform exit while I commandeer a taxi – this has now become like a military operation as every second counts. Finally, a cab becomes available just as I see from the arrivals board the train is in, perfect! But no, there is no sign of Christopher or Mr Waller – I bribe the driver to wait and rush back into the station where I find them strolling down the platform and of course he was coming from right from the very back carriage!

Trying to remain calm and diplomatic (this is the first time we have met), I attempt to step things up a little while Mr Waller suggests picking up a coffee – what the ****! Once in the cab I call ahead to Ken Bruce's producer who tells me they only have the studio until 1 pm – it is now nearly noon which was our due arrival time. Luckily the driver is good and fast, the traffic kind and we roll up, albeit on the wrong side of the road of the BBC entrance, just after mid-day so good to go… phew.

Following this traumatic start to my time with the legendary singer songwriter, things improve and the pre-recorded interview goes well (eventually goes to air on February 23, 2010) although too late for the Christmas album I am plugging, it is Ken's 'album of the week'. That same December afternoon, Christopher is also interviewed by Steve Wright who also gives *Christmas Time Is Here* a great plug, live on air.

The day just gets better as the Jazz Cafe gig also gets a great radio plug and the show is simply sensational – a full house was guaranteed. I pick up again with Christopher the following year for promotion of his 'Doctor Faith' album and again in 2016 for the re-release of his *Cafe Carlyle Sessions* – he proved to be a popular guest with the radio stations throughout the years. However it is often a problem when an artist who has massive success some 30 years previously introduces new music to the world which really only wants to hear those hits – *Sailing*, *Ride Like The Wind*, *Arthurs Them* etc. were all rolled out again and again while the new songs struggled to get an airing. 'Cafe Carlyle' consisted of acoustic re-recordings of his hits but stations quite understandably preferred to play the original versions.

It is usually the plugger that gets the blame. By this time, Christopher's albums were being released by German based Edel Records on their ear MUSIC imprint, still run today by Max Vaccaro and in my meetings with him at the MIDEM music festival in Cannes and again in London, it transpired that they were looking to refresh their UK operation including distribution and marketing. I recommended an indie company, Absolute who went on to handle the German company's entire catalogue and a nice retainer deal was on the table for me to look after all their radio and TV interests. Absolute were offered the deal; I suffered the consequences of Christopher Cross' lack of UK sales, so between them they found another plugger – an occupational hazard.

As for Christopher himself, I found him nice enough and there is no doubting his voice is genuinely unique – that amazing high-range reaching notes that for most male singers is impossible. However, when it came to his personality there was no real 'sparkle' – I think for him it was just about the songs, the records and nothing else.

Chapter 29
Jools Holland

With Jools and American Jazz singer, Aubrey Logan at the Helicon Mountain Studios, Greenwich – September 18, 2017

Jools is a key figure in the music industry with his TV show 'Later' running over 25 years and occasional Radio 2 series, both featuring the widest possible range of music throughout. However, in the end he is a truly down-to-earth musician, a piano player with no apparent ego or hidden agenda – extraordinary given the massive influence he has over the business. Every band and artist in the world dreams about an appearance on his show. Of course he has his own 'rhythm and blues orchestra', constantly touring and releasing over 40 albums over a 40-year period.

Jools started his recording career with Squeeze in 1974 – original members Chris Difford and Glen Tilbrook have kept it going to this day.

He then became co-presenter with Paula Yates, of the iconic TV series 'The Tube' for five years from 1982 – seen possibly as the forerunner to the only present day music TV show, 'Later With Jools'!

I have been fortunate enough to be a regular visitor to Jools' own studio in Greenwich, Helicon Mountain (designed with influences from Portmeirion/The

Prisoner TV series), taking in various artists to record his Radio 2 series (see earlier the Marc Almond session). Others include Ronnie Wood, Graham Gouldman (lOcc), Holly Johnson, Justin Hayward, Rick Wakeman, Gary Brooker (Procol Harum), Roger McGough (The Scaffold), Nicky Haslam (designer), Jimmy Somerville, Rick Wakeman, Bob Stanley (Saint Etienne) and new Jazz/Pop artist, Aubrey Logan (who sings and plays trombone)!

Chapter 30
Radio DJs

From the BBC's Light Programme where Terry Wogan set out on his illustrious career in the UK, through to today's stars such as Chris Evans and Dermot O'Leary – I have dealt with them all in one way or another.

It is probably not common knowledge, that in main, it is not the presenters who choose the tracks they play but of course they can significantly influence radio playlists. My current priority station is BBC Radio 2 who operate a strict rotation system on their daytime shows so only a handful of DJ's have any choice – Jo Whiley is one of the few 'influencers' and the 'specialists' such as Trevor Nelson/Craig Charles (soul/funk), Bob Harris (country), Cerys Matthews (blues) etc. There was a time when those such as Alex Lester, Janice Long and that legend, Terry Wogan would love to champion new artists but for one reason or another, they are no longer with the station. Radio 1 and 6 Music do take more notice of DJs choices, but again daytime airplay is mainly taken from a set playlist. Commercial radio is totally dictated by the advertisers so it implements a very rigid system – commonly known as a 'Top 40' rotation policy.

When Bob Harris hosted his Saturday night show, he was totally open to being plugged with new artists – he was totally driven by the music. I have had a long and pleasant relationship with Bob, a totally dedicated professional. Terry Wogan became one of the biggest names in radio and TV but I always found him approachable and would always listen favourably to my new releases – he particularly liked the singer-songwriter genre.

One of my best friends, Duncan Johnson was in the original Radio 1 line up and he later helped to launch Capital Radio. I could always call him to talk about my latest releases, a situation that ran right through to his retirement from radio in 1988 although our friendship endured until he sadly passed away in 2018.

Duncan Johnson at Capital Radio 1980

Likewise, I struck up a wonderful relationship with Alex Lester, his dedication to music so impressed and his style is so appealing! I had some memorable times with Alex from his early days at Radio 2 until this day while he is broadcasting for Greatest Hits Radio, part of the Bauer Radio Group. When Radio 2 let him go after 22 years, he continued working with the BBC on several of their regional stations and hosted the breakfast show for the West Midlands for over two years. But it was BBC Radio Oxford, where he had free choice on his weekly Friday afternoon show. I was honoured to become a regular guest there when Alex would interview me about my experiences and for a change I could play three tracks of my choice – a dream come true for any plugger.

With Alex Lester at one of my regular visits to BBC Radio Oxford.

May 2016

I knew Chris Evans from his time in local radio but when he moved in next door to our Golden Square offices we would hang out in the local pubs and bars but rarely spoke music. It was all about 'personality' with him and he pretty much invented 'Zoo Radio' – plenty of fast banter. To his credit he knew how to do a deal having bought and then sold Virgin Radio at a huge personal profit. When he finally landed at Radio 2 he seemed to have energy in abundance and was determined to show he could still do it, but he still remembered his old friends.

However, although he meant well his false promises were disappointing – he would ask me what I was working on and then said he would, "Play it tomorrow," – maybe he did play it but not on air.

With Chris Evans following Dodgy's live appearance on his Radio 2
breakfast show, July 2016

Generally, I have enjoyed some fantastic times with some of the best DJs in the business – perhaps the '80s being the most memorable. The Radio 1 Roadshows usually involved an overnight stay as the show would go to air at around mid-day and it was the time of Gary Davies, Mike Read, Adrian Juste, Steve Wright, Simon Bates, Simon Mayo, Dave Lee Travis, Tony Blackburn, Johnnie Walker and perhaps the most influential of them all, John Peel although he was not really at home with the Roadshow's frivolity.

Meanwhile, Capital Radio was probably at its peak in that decade too and had the best in Mick Brown, Pat Sharp and Neil Fox. It is pleasing that most of these guys are still friends to this day although others, not so much. I have always thought that a dedicated radio DJ suffers from being in a darkened studio and not being able to see their audience which can present itself as a form of shyness – only coming to life when the microphone is switched on. BBC Radio London's Robert Elms is a case in point. I have been a guest on his show many times but found it impossible to engage him outside of the studio. In the street, in a bar or a shop – total blank but next time – back on air – friends again. In more recent times I have come to admire the BBC 6 Music line up who seem to put music first and are incredibly knowledgeable. Gideon Coe, Shaun Keaveny, Steve Lamacq and Chris Hawkins are particular favourites of mine and not just because they occasionally play my records.

Chapter 31
Radio and Television Producers

The most important contacts for any plugger, promoter or PR!

Where to start on this subject – it is potentially endless, having dealt with so many producers over so many years, but here's how I found them:

Starting in 1966 my first assignment was to visit the BBC's Aeolian Hall studios in New Bond Street, the most amazing building which became a radio studio in 1943 facilitating producers working on the Light Programme's live music broadcasts. Ian Fenner was the first producer I met, taking in a Russ Conway record on vinyl of course in those days. Such a nice man who said he would play it on his 'Round Midnight' show.

When Radio 1 launched the following year, Aeolian Hall became their base for live music along with Radio 2 with some shows being broadcast on both networks. Radio 1 also used Egton House, near Broadcasting House in Portland Place, named the 'Grams' department as the shows here only featured (gramophone) records.

Keen to meet as many producers as possible, I would hang out at nearby Terry's club – a rather sleazy drinking club frequented by various music publishers, pluggers and producers. Terry was a larger than life lady who made the best steak and kidney pie and her husband, Eric was related to the infamous Kray twins.

I became very friendly with producer Malcolm Brown, a relationship which lasted until he retired in 1996 when the station had a 'review' clean up with many producers given early retirement. His first job was as a junior assistant producer on the David Symonds' drive time show and I managed to secure plenty of airplay thanks to Malcolm with some help from Symonds himself. The executive producer was known for his aggressive attitude – this unpopular man was Ron Belchier. He verbally abused everyone and saw pluggers as a soft target, reducing some (literally) to tears. I managed to hold my own as he once challenged me to read some sheet music and asked what key a certain track was played in – I passed both tests and indeed as I was still working with sheet music as well as records, gifted him copies for his daughter who was learning piano.

Although challenging, these were fun times – we would all meet in the BBC basement canteen, the local pub, as well as Terry's club to compare notes and generally help each other. I also bumped into Muff Winwood (brother of Steve) who had recently left the Spencer Davies Group to work for Island Records and was filling in as their plugger – he would actually ask for my help which I found very flattering considering I was still learning myself.

After a few years, most producers moved to Egton House which became the headquarters of a completely autonomous Radio 1, with Aeolian Hall becoming the home of Radio 2 before moving to Charlotte Street some time later.

By the 1970s, Radio 1 had built up tremendous power being the only national radio station playing pop music all day being supplied by an increasingly competitive and potentially lucrative record business. This power was very much abused by many producers – the aforementioned Ron Belchier, Ted Beston (Jimmy Saville's long standing, or falling producer), Paul Williams (who was one time head of their playlist committee) were the biggest offenders. Others were more reasonable and some are still friends to this day – Roger Pusey, who at the time produced the all-powerful Tony Blackburn breakfast show was always good and fair to deal with and Bill Bebb who produced *Saturday Club* and *Easy Beat* was wonderful – a friend right up until his passing in 2016. He came through the ranks of radio producers who actually produced live sessions so were required to have a comprehensive musical and technical knowledge. Bill conducted live sessions with many of the great 60s' bands including Jimi Hendrix, Cream, The Who, The Small Faces etc. Today, no such talent is required and musical knowledge is thought of as having the recall of how many hits that Abba had plus other such stats!

BILL BEBB – a legend of the BBC & truly talented radio producer.

It was around this time I first met my career long friend, Phil Swern who was also on the plugging circuit but turned record producer in 1970 with a Top 20 hit by Horace Faith, *Black Pearl*. A string of hits followed by The Pearls, Polly Brown and R and J Stone, but then Phil joined the production staff of Radio 1, responsible for Pick Of The Pops which much later transferred to Radio 2. Other shows followed and in particular the record review programme, 'Roundtable' which he loved as he was sent every single release by record companies. He also produced Bob Harris first shows for Radio 1 which again made the transition to Radio 2 at the turn of the millennium. During the '90s, Phil produced shows for Capital Radio and Capital Gold. As if this is not sufficient, Phil built up a massive record collection including every UK Top 40 single since 1952. The collection is now run as a business with his partner, Andy Hill's company, 'I Like Music'. Such an unassuming gentleman who almost doesn't belong in the music business, but he has achieved so much at a top level – he even compiles the questions for Ken Bruce's 'Popmaster' and has produced numerous radio and TV quiz shows.

Phil had a few years as part of Radio 2's all important playlist committee and it was a very big moment for me was when he single headedly pushed Lisbee Stainton's *Red* on to their playlist in December 2008 which kick-started a good career for her. To celebrate this achievement her father and manager, Clive asked me to organise an evening at the BBC Club which proved a huge success. Lisbee went on to play the 02 Arena, several festivals and supported Joan Armatrading on a world tour which included a show at London's Royal Albert Hall. The Staintons were such a joy to work with and although Lisbee was never a superstar, she did have a long successful career.

I managed to convince Robert Elms about her talent and she played live on his show many times including live from the Olympic Park in 2012.

Lisbee Stainton outside the Robert Elms studio at the Olympic Park – August 2012

Meanwhile back at Radio 2, how things changed with Phil no longer involved in the playlist and the passing of Terry Wogan in 2016, leaving no one to champion the upcoming British singer/songwriter. Terry's legacy is well but Phil is one of the somewhat unrecognised major contributors to broadcasting over a generation and I consider myself very fortunate to have had him as a friend for over 50 years.

PHIL SWERN (1st on left) with Annette Barrett, Rell Lafargue
(both Reservoir-Reverb Music at the MPA Christmas lunch 2013)

Then there was Radio Luxembourg 208! I Even before those rebel pirate stations opened up in 1964, we teenagers would listen in our bedrooms to the 'Station Of The Stars' as the only way to hear the new releases, although transmitting from the far away Grand Duchy, the signal was always poor and it could be very frustrating when suddenly The Beatles would sound like Daleks on the chorus of *She Loves You*!

They were the first ever commercial radio station with most sponsors being the record companies, so initially it was extremely difficult to obtain 'free plays'! Of course the pirates changed that and things opened up – even more so when Radio 1 started in 1967. It was never that clear how important they were in the overall scheme of things but all the staff were a delight to deal with, especially programme director, Ken Evans. He would always host a meeting with pluggers and pretty much would give every record presented at least ONE spin. If it was a real contender, he was forced to suggest a deal whereby their publishing company, Louvigny-Marquee would take the B side thus guaranteeing a 'Power Play' – elsewhere on these pages I mentioned an occasion when Mickie Most gave away MY B side without permission.

Countless DJs gained useful experience on 208 – Barry Aldiss was one of their first resident DJs in the '60s before joining the BBC – he was a close friend of my one time boss at Noel Gay so he would hang out in the office before we all went to the pub where most of the 'work' was done; the 'Royal Ruler', Tony Prince was the most memorable in that decade, a true legend; Alan Freeman had a regular show but his main work initially from the BBC's Light Programme when he came over from his native Melbourne – there were so many but I also remember Paul Burnett, Mark Wesley who joined much later and of course the amiable DJ, the DJ, Duncan Johnson.

Any airplay helps and sometimes some Radio Lux coverage could save a pluggers skin but it was Radio 1 that really counted and for 20 years many of the staff took undue advantage of their position! I remember one of their high profile DJ's (who is still up there but currently at Radio 2) saying that his producer was promoted beyond his capabilities… I thought a little harsh at the time but looking back, he definitely had a point. However, there was much fun to be had on the Radio 1 Roadshows although there was a time when, rather arrogantly they spurned the chance of booking artists as they considered the DJs to be the stars – the public was eventually spared the dubious privilege of staring at the likes of Simon Bates, Gary Davies, Noel Edmunds etc., not doing much at all. The flood gates opened once Kylie and Jason brought in multi thousands on various beaches around the UK! Originally the roadshows were devised by producer, Johnny Beerling who went on to become Radio 1 controller in 1985, a position he retained until he was forced into early retirement in 1993 – part of John Bill's massive shake up. For a while I commuted into central London with him – an hour long train ride seemed endless when he forced me to listen to their new jingles package! His son David was my paperboy before going on to slightly better things becoming Director of the Leverhulme Centre for climate change and has written three books on plant and animal sciences!

Johnny Beerling –
Radio 1 Controller 1985–93

With Clare Marvin at Radio One reception,
Yalding House their home in the millennium
years. Clare has been with the station longer
than anyone, serving a remarkable 35 years.
No one enters without her permission!

Capital Radio became the first commercial station to compete with the BBC when it opened its doors in October 1973 and there was a more welcoming feeling about the place with DJs including my friend Duncan Johnson, Dave Cash, Roger Scott, Tommy Vance, Kenny Everett etc proving a strong opposition to the cheesy Radio 1 team. Their producers would welcome input from pluggers and were very open – Tim Blackmore, Aiden Day, Jon Myer, Mike Childs, Annie O'Neill. Clive Smith were all great to deal with and became good friends. Later, DJs Mick Brown, Pat Sharp, Neil Fox moved the station on to another level but were always approachable.

TOP MAN – DJ MICK BROWN

Unfortunately, commercial radio today has become rigidly formatted, somewhat sanitised while the BBC has come right back into its own, at least as far as opportunities for artists and musicians is concerned. Radio 1 targets a young audience but still includes live music in their schedules, while Radio 2 go for the 25 year olds (and rising) providing a vast variety of music, features, documentaries, live concerts along with sister station, 6 Music whose output is unlike any station that has come before it – just so interesting, anything good goes but largely 'Indie'!

Producers working at both 2 and 6 are a plugger's dream – all friendly and approachable but most importantly recognising that we have an important role to play in their output.

The last 15 years when these stations really flourished have probably been the most enjoyable for me with spending so much time with producers such as Henry Lopez (Gideon Coe's producer), Andy Warrell (various shows on 2 and 6), Michael Banbrook (R2 music team), Anthony Dunning/Paul Mann/Tom Fenner (Steve Wright), Julie Newman (various on 2), Mark Hagen (Jools Holland/Bob Harris), Al Booth, Anthony Cherry, Bridget Apps (Radio 2 live music but now retired) plus many more, made my job so much of a pleasure, whether or not I could achieve my aims!

Many presenters successfully crossed over from Radio 1 – Steve Wright becoming the first and possibly the most successful but Zoe Ball, Jo Whiley and Sara Cox all coming a close second. 6 Music, predominantly line up musicians to present key shows including Lauren Laverne, Tom Robinson, Cerys Matthews and Iggy Pop!

BBC Radio London came into its own as an outlet for artists, new and established – especially over the last 20 years, well really since Robert Elms took to their airwaves in 1994. Graham Robertson was their brilliant researcher for most of this time and we became close friends following my regular visits to the station which was then based in Marylebone High Street, conveniently located close to my London base.

Graham loves his music and is incredibly intuitive – a real enthusiast too and would attend gigs nearly every evening with a view to checking out the best artists for Robert Elms. A rare quality as he was happy to go to a dingy east end pub as well as Wembley or the 02 Arena – the most regular haunts would be the Barfly and the Dublin Castle in Camden, the rather unusual setting of St Pancras Old Church. I could also rely on him to support my regular showcases at the BBC Club and on several occasions he would 'sell' my acts to Robert resulting in a live session plus interview on the show. Graham worked across the board at the station – Danny Baker, Gary Crowley and Sean Rowley were just a few of his presenters. Unfortunately, Graham returned home to Liverpool for family reasons and is seriously missed. However, Robert's long standing main producer, Sarah Bateson is great to deal with and a lovely person all round.

I have mentioned earlier that a strange kind of 'barrier' exists between some DJs and the record industry – maybe it's a form of shyness but in spite of my countless visits to the Robert Elms show over many years, and indeed my own guests slots where it was just the two of us in the room, it is difficult to really get to know him, a consummate professional but on a personal level, a 'cold fish'! On the other hand, Gary Crowley is a warm sincere person who also really knows his music – he is/was a Mod, so all good by me!

With Radio 2's Mark Hagen at a Jools Holland Show recording

TV

TV Centre in 2019, now home to ITV's daytime programmes. As BBC TV Centre from 1960 to 2013 it staged the famous 'Top of the Pops' until 1994 when it moved to Borehamwood.

TV plugging requires a different set of skills and over the years, major record companies would employ TV 'specialists' in vast numbers.

Today there are far less opportunities for music on terrestrial TV – the only designated music show is 'Later With Jools' produced by the irreplaceable Mark Cooper and Alison Howe. Previously we had 'Ready Steady Go' (63–66), 'The Old Grey Whistle Test' (71–88) and 'The Tube' (82–87, co-presented by Jools with Paula Yates), the all-powerful 'Top of the Pops' which was based on the Top 40 singles chart, countless children's shows, featuring plenty of music, including 'Razzamatazz', 'Going Live', 'Motormouth', 'Ghost Train', 'Tiswas', 'Supersonic', 'Live and Kicking', 'Wide Awake Club' etc. We still have daytime shows to plug but music is generally the poor relation whereas in its infancy for example, TVAM was full of plugging opportunities, famously with 'Mad Lizzy' and her morning work outs.

The priorities are very different in that the sound comes second – it is mainly about the visuals so certain types of artists have an advantage – we certainly did when it came to the very attractive Kylie, Jason, Sinitta, etc.

As much of these shows output was 'live', producers and researchers would always give priority to the most reliable artists (and pluggers come to that).

Of course the big shows want the big stars – Des O'Connor Tonight had ratings of around 20 million at one time. Producer Brian Penders was an eccentric character, always telling jokes (or "gags" as he like to say) and main researcher, Sean Murphy was a joy to deal with but we could forget about pitching any new artists. Des's show was the last of a long history of 'light entertainment' shows, often early Saturday evening fodder plus the magical 'Sunday Night At The London Palladium' which hosted every major international star of a generation.

I was with Des O'Connor at a movie star themed fancy dress party in 2005 – I went as Steve McQueen; not sure who Des was but he still just looked like Des O'Connor!

Generally, it felt as if TV producers had more respect for pluggers and acknowledged that we had an important role to play – the process was so much more than just handing out records. Being London based most of my contacts came from within the BBC TV Centre and the London South Bank studios but Tyne Tees TV in Newcastle certainly made its mark with The Tube, Razzamatazz and The White Room. One of the best was Chris Cowey who followed Ric Blaxill as Top of the Pops producer in 1997 – a really warm hearted, friendly 'Geordie' who never abused his position. In 1994 Sharp End sponsored a premier league football game against Newcastle so we used the opportunity to invite a few of the Tyne Tees TV guys to be our guests. As a Sunderland supporter, Chris Cowey declined. A four-two defeat meant that manager, Kevin Keegan would not allow any of his team to join us as man of the match, so we chose two players from Wimbledon, Peter Fear and Vinnie Jones (both seen below) holding their champagne award. A splendid time was had by all. Others included below are Tilly Rutherford (PWL), Duncan Johnson (DJ), Dave Mackie (Disctronics) and Ric Blaxill, more of him later.

Cathy Gilbey was the 'don' of children's TV and booked the artists for the BBCs 'Multi Coloured Swap Show', 'Going Live' and 'Live and Kicking' so, all-powerful but she was always very fair. Happy memories of lunches at the nearby Shepherd's Bush Kensington Hilton's Japanese Restaurant – two occasions in particular: Waiting for our table, Cathy started to tell us how upset she was with Robbie Williams as he had let her down with an appearance the coming Saturday morning. As the Sake went down, this became louder, more repetitive and continued as, my old friend David Enthoven arrived and sat a couple of tables away – he was Robbie's manager and had heard it all. He reacted in true style and grace – fortunately he had a great sense of humour.

On another occasion, Cathy became more and more animated over something and the chopsticks started getting out of control – the plastic type, had great tolerance and bent back before pinging forward striking another customer in the head. Cathy didn't take a breath and in fact tucked in to my left over beef, only to repeat the trick.

CATHY GILBEY – BBC CHILDREN'S TV PRODUCER

PAUL CIANI (2ⁿᵈ from right) in Central Park, NYC 1989

Also with me and Robert Lemon are an unknown prize winner (left) and
DJ STEVE WRIGHT (far right)

My closest TV contacts, who over time became good friends were Paul Ciani, one-time 'Top Of The Pops' producer and Maurice Gallagher who started as an assistant floor manager at the BBC but ended his career as Head Of Entertainment for GMTV at its height of success.

Paul sadly left for the big TV in the sky in 1991; Maurice is a good friend and neighbour to this day.

Ric Blaxill is the only music producer who has enjoyed a long and successful career in BOTH radio and television!

I first met Ric in the Yorkshire Grey pub near Radio 1 on the day he started as a trainee in 1988 and we immediately hit it off, especially when it came to football talk, although he is an Arsenal supporter (along with Robert Lemon).

He certainly has had some jobs during his 32-year career. Making his mark at Radio 1 where his youthful energy broke the mould of the tired old men. However, even then there were signs that his success was affecting his attitude, especially when he achieved the top job of producing the breakfast show.

At this point Ric asked us to organise the entertainment for his wedding – a dubious task as these occasions carry a very mixed audience. He really wanted something unusual and boy did he get it! Robert and I were good friends of record men, Nigel Reveller and Colin Jennings who fronted a 'comedy' routine band, 'Star Turn On 45 Pints' – absolutely hilarious but part of the joke was to conduct a meat raffle which horrified Ric's new wife so we had to rapidly withdraw this part.

In 1994 when 'Top of the Pops' was featuring more and more of our artists, he was given the producers job but he had absolutely no knowledge in this area so he summoned me and Robert (Lemon) to lunch at TV Centre for a serious consultation session. Some vintage port ended the meal (and the day) but we paid the bill of course! This was a tough job for Ric as with the benefit of hindsight, the show had already passed its best days but he had a good crack at it.

However, it was disappointing that, given our relationship, he gave us a really hard time on some occasions. We hung on in there and after every show we would take him for a curry at the nearby Eastern Brasserie in Elstree – we had no idea how much all this would pay off for us!

In 1998 Ric struck a deal with London Weekend TV to devise and launch a new Saturday morning TV series fronted by Ant and Dec, CDUK/SMTV – Sharp End was engaged as the PR company on a very lucrative contract! We organised a big launch party and attended Friday evening rehearsal, Saturday morning live and post/pre-production meetings on Monday mornings. This continued nicely for the best part of a year but after a while we noticed that Ric was hardly around – TV politics had set in with executive producer, Conor McAnally wanting him out.

They finally ended our contract and appointed the corporate Freud Communications but over time it proved we had done the job.

Ric's next TV show was 'Friday Night's All Wright' hosted by Ric's footballing hero, Ian Wright. Something unusual happened; he booked me for the show to appear as a football referee!

Here was the set up – in the first show a cage was installed on the set, full of Spurs supporters so Ian could occasionally circle them to wind them up. In this episode there were 30 referees' all in their black, along with me was Premier League man, Roger Milford who famously did not send off Paul Gascoigne when he ruptured his cruciate ligament after a wild tackle early in the FA cup final. So with Lennox Lewis as our security guard, we were only released if we performed the 'Men In Black' dance routine. Even after several hours' rehearsal, it was a complete shambles so we were locked in for the entire one hour – not that painful with Shania Twain as one of the guests to enjoy.

After the show, executive producer, Bob Massie bought us all a drink and gave us the 'props' of Ray-Ban sunglasses in lieu of a fee. I originally met Bob when he produced 'Six O'clock Live' and I accompanied many star guests into his office which served as the green room. More recently I have been reunited with him as he was also executive producer of a Kylie Minogue documentary (see Radio and TV appearances) but now happy in retirement as a Wycombe Wanderers supporter.

Ric returned to radio in 2001 as creative director for an early digital service (Stormlive) before joining Capital Radio as group creative director and then moved on to launch BBC 6 Music in 2004 as head of programmes with my old friend from early days of Capital, Jon Myer appointed head of music. These were defining moments as this station was my number one 'go to' network, especially when I started working the Cherry Red catalogue in 2005 as most of their product is the perfect fit.

Finally Ric joined Bauer Media in 2007 (to date) as their music and content director for its radio division – these stations include Absolute, Kiss, Magic, Planet Rock, Kerrang, Scala and several regionals.

As I have said, this man certainly has had some jobs!

Robert and I with Dutch pop band, 2 Unlimited and Ric Blaxill (centre) at a lunch to celebrate a million sales of *No Limit* – significantly Ric was first to programme the single in the R1 breakfast show.

Chapter 32
Other Experiences

Journalism – Record World Magazine

By the end of the 1960s it felt like the music industry had truly come of age and the American market was massive, just off the scale. The record companies had always considered Billboard magazine as the 'bible' and it was their charts that defined success; Cash Box was a poor number two until Record World exploded on to the scene – it went on to almost take over Billboard's crown. The owners, Sid Parnes and Bob Austin were represented by Noel Gay's American attorneys who in turn suggested that I should become their UK correspondent.

Bob Austin visited London to give me my brief which was to supply a weekly column and naming two singles and an album of British origin that I tipped for American success. Suddenly all the music PRs were inviting me to lunch, receptions, concerts and launch parties but best of all was to be on the mailing lists of every record company, receiving every release in a rich decade for music.

I was able to fulfil my weekly commitment quite well along with my music publishing duties but I did not then expect to be thrown in at the deep end to make major contributions to several 'advertorials' commencing with The Who, one of my favourite bands of the time. The band's PR, Keith Altham immediately set up an interview with Pete Townshend! This was to be my debut in this role but I was a little comforted by the fact I was a genuine fan so had plenty of background although I invested several hours in preparing the questions. Arriving at Pete's house in Teddington, West London I was surprised that he answered the door himself and made me very welcome. I apprehensively pressed the start button on my tape machine and went for it, the rest was easy with Pete being so eloquent and expansive with his answers. In fact, I only managed four questions from around 24 as he gave me everything I needed and more. He also offered up the exclusive use in the feature of a picture hanging on his toilet wall.

Pete Townshend's picture as printed in Record World Magazine in 1974,
straight from his toilet wall.

The finished feature comprised six pages in this very special 100-page edition published on November 23, 1974. One quote from Pete: "I think the most satisfying thing overall has been 'Quadrophenia' as a piece, because I saw that through from the beginning – the writing, I controlled all that, I did all the recording and the mixing and looked after the cover."

This adventure was an incredible thrill having followed the band since the beginning, 10 years earlier and had queued for hours to catch them at various pubs and clubs around London including several visits to the legendary Marquee Club in London's Wardour Street. But it was a performance at the Wimbledon Palais that made an everlasting impression when they destroyed their equipment to spectacular effect – I later discovered that everything was reassembled overnight to be reused as they only had two sets of gear!

PICTURE PRESENT: The Marquee Club – my regular haunt to see the bands of

the day including THE WHO, SMALL FACES,
JIMI HENDRIX and THE ROLLING STONES

As part of the project I also interviewed Roger Daltry and John Entwistle along with management representatives and some of the road crew (John Wolff, production manager and Bob Pridden, sound engineer) responsible for recycling their equipment. Roger's most poignant, fate tempting quote was, "There is no chance of our ever breaking up and as far as I'm concerned, we haven't done anything yet, we haven't created anything and tomorrow is Day One, that's how we go on."

Sadly, Keith Moon passed away just four years later and John Entwistle left us in 2002.

Such a success, other advertorials followed on an annual basis: The Bee Gees in 1975, which included an interview with Robert Stigwood; then Elton John, with a highlight being a conversation with producer, Gus Dudgeon (but the rest I have written in a songwriter's section later); finally Deep Purple was the subject in 1977.

Having built something of a reputation as a journalist, I was commissioned by the UK trade magazine, MUSIC WEEK to compile a special tribute to the hard rock band, Nazareth to celebrate their 10th anniversary. This involved a flight to Edinburgh where one of the band picked me up to drive to their house in their home town of Dunfirmline where I would conduct a comprehensive interview with the whole band. Although they never reached the heights of some of their contemporaries, the band, fronted by the charismatic Dan McCafferty, did have hit singles with *Broken Down Angel, This Flight Tonight, My White Bicycle* and *Bad Bad Boy* and released over 20 albums during a 40-year career, so there was plenty to discuss. I found them extremely helpful and friendly so we made a good start over coffee before the malt whiskey was produced, quickly followed by a trip to their local pub for lunch. Thankfully I recorded everything and had just about enough material before things degenerated into a haze of heavy drinking. I vaguely remember being driven to the airport and poured onto a plane before I passed out completely.

Radio and TV Appearances

My radio debut was on LBC in the 1970s as part of a campaign to save Denmark Street, threatened by the property developers of the day. This was followed by some filming in my office there for a BBC TV documentary about record promotion, 'The Persuaders'.

I have much more detailed memories of my several interviews on BBC Radio London's Robert Elms Show, particular when I became the subject of his 'Listed Londoner' on November 5, 2012. Not exactly fireworks but an interesting exchange with Robert as I was consistently swinging the conversation around to my current record releases, whilst Mr Elms continually brought it back on script talking about things such as my favourite London landmarks, restaurants, venue, pubs etc. As a nod to my sheet music days, my walk on track was Edith PiafFs *La Vie En Rose* chosen by my good friend, producer, Graham Robertson but I thought the Grace Jones version would have been cooler.

I happened to be visiting the station on the day that famous songwriter, Jerry Leiber died so I was invited straight on air to deliver a tribute. Fortunately, I had worked with him only a few years earlier and one of his great Elvis Presley stories was fresh in my mind.

Another honour was to be invited on to the show as part of the BBC's vinyl week when they staged an OB (outside broadcast) at the old EMI factory in Hayes, West London. Back in the day part of any promo campaign would be to take the artist to meet and greet the factory staff. I relayed on air the story of Reg Matthews, the then factory manager who refused to accept an order for coloured vinyl for the Motorhead album – "Vinyl is black," was his response but we won him over in the end.

To my surprise, Reg was also a guest on the show so I had to be careful and went on the diplomatic rather than controversial route (Reg was too old school for me and he could frustrate our ambitions). As part of this vinyl week I was also asked to undertake several interviews for the BBC regional stations, all done by an ISDN link from Wogan House in London. The sheer repetition of most of the questions made me realise what artists had to contend with on a regular basis but I quickly developed a technique of devising interesting and different answers.

Robert Elms on my right at the old EMI factory and distribution centre, Hayes, London

As previously mentioned, I had long admired DJ Alex Lester during his long spell at Radio 2 and shared his taste in music, so I jumped at the chance of becoming a regular guest on his Friday afternoon show at BBC Radio Oxford. During a 30-minute slot I would relay my stories but always followed a theme. For example, one show it was all about the seventies so I was able to bring in a new single by Slade's Jim Lea and another regular client, Graham Gouldman from 10cc; another was the 'alternative '80s so the Blow Monkeys fitted in perfectly; then we had the great songwriters when I chose songs by Burt Bacharach, Tony Macaulay, Jamie Hartman (*Human* by Rag 'n' Bone Man) and new singer-songwriter, Hannah's Yard. Two Christmas specials included past seasonal No 1's of my choice including my own *Lily The Pink* by The Scaffold.

One of my most challenging radio interviews was about the Flamingo Club, a cool jazz/blues venue during the '60s and '70s when Georgie Fame had a residency. Now Radio 2 producer, Carmela di Clemente was recording a mini documentary about the club for transmission during the interval of a 'Friday Night Is Music Night' edition coming live from the Cheltenham Jazz festival, starring George Fame. The club owner, Jeff Kruger was not available as he lived in Miami but did record a short piece for the show. My problem was I had only visited the venue on three or four occasions (the Marquee was my preferred choice back then) but Carmella had engaged me as the main spokesperson as I was the only one she knew who had been there at all. Fortunately, as well as Georgie, I had seen my favourite mod bands, The Small Faces and The Creation play there which at least gave me something to go on. Carmella wanted as much material as possible so I did some online research to back up my own memories – just as well as the interview just ran and ran.

The Flamingo Club, the 'in club' for live music in the '60s.

In 2012, I appeared on a Stock, Aitken Waterman documentary for ITV where my main contribution was in describing the circumstance surround the start of Kylie and Jason's careers. Pete Waterman also participated but not Mike Stock or Matt Aitken.

Screen shot from the S.A.W. ITV documentary.

A few years later I was approached to participate in a Kylie Minogue TV documentary celebrating her 50th birthday which was produced by my old friend from ITV, Bob Massie who had now joined production company, IMG. Coincidently their studios in Stockley Park, West London also houses the controversial VAR decision review system for the Premier Football League.

I described my role in her career during Kylie's five years with PWL and further year with BMG's Deconstruction label and how that transition evolved with such difficulty.

KYLIE AT 50: ESPECIALLY FOR YOU

9.00PM, SUNDAY 13TH MAY 2018

A SPECIAL 90' DOCUMENTARY CELEBRATING KYLIE'S 50TH BIRTHDAY AND THE 30TH ANNIVERSARY OF HER FIRST UK HIT

Executive Producer for IMG Productions - Bob Massie
Head of Production - Jane Tetthull
Development Executive - Jess Pack
Producer/Director - Martin Smith
Producer - Simon Broadley
Archive Producer - Andrew Wright
Editors - Isobel Gostrick and John MacDonald
Production Manager - Julian Adams
Production Secretary - LB Ronnie Carter
Commissioning Editor for Channel 5 - Greg Barnett

Chapter 33
Music Awards Shows/
Festivals Including Midem.

Ivor Novello's

Probably the most prestigious of all awards shows for over 60 years – I have attended around half of these and enjoyed success with Tony Macauley who was 'Songwriter Of The Year' in the seventies on two occasions. I also ran the PR campaign for the legendary songwriter/producer team of Jerry Lieber and Mike Stoller in 2001. The same year (good friend), Pam Sheyne won with *Genie In A Bottle*.

My ad in Music Week when MD of Noel Gay Music & below

Pictured with Lieber & Stoller (seated), winners of "Special International Award" 2001 & their publishers Rondor Music staff, MD Richard Thomas (seated centre)

Pam Sheyne (hit songwriter including "Genie In A Bottle"),
Eddie Levy (music publisher) and Ron McCreight-Grosvenor House Hotel 2017

Music Week

Throughout 1988–9, we at Sharp End Promotions had worked on over 40 Top 40 singles (including eight No 1's) and seven Top 5 albums. In addition to massive TV coverage, at any one time we enjoyed 10 tracks over the Radio 1 and Capital Radio playlists! However, when it came to the Music Week 'Plugger Of The Year' awards the votes were not "weighted" – a vote from the 10 million rated Radio 1 had the same value as a vote from any of the 100 regional stations whose ratings and impact were minimal. Therefore it was given that a regional plugger would always win and in particular it was always Bob Herman as he worked for the CBS corporation (now Sony). Eventually, even he seemed embarrassed.

I have always considered myself a good loser but, of all the awards given out, I really thought that this was one myself and Robert Lemon deserved, being untouchable in terms of success at this time.

Not strictly an awards show (although they usually present out one or two) – the Music Publishers Association's Christmas lunch is another essential annual event and I have attended most over the past 50 years.

The picture below taken at the 1990 bash features from me to the left:

Paul Williams, Ted Beston (both Radio 1 producers), Sue Foster (Sharp End PR), Malcolm Brown, Roger Pusey (both Radio 1), David Howells (PWL Records MD), Adrian Williams (RCA Head of Promotion), Peter Powell (DJ), Pete Waterman and Chris Lycett (Radio 1)

These Radio 1 producers represented almost total power over their all-important playlist at the time!

The BMI Awards

BMI is an American royalty collection agency who have a major presence in the UK – they are responsible for hosting this annual event staged at London's Dorchester Hotel.

Thanks to my friendships with the UK managers, initially Phil Graham and then Brandon Baski, I have been invited on several occasions. This is a chance to rub shoulders with some song writing legends and performers. Graham Gouldman was honoured in 2015 (already pictured) – others have included Steve Winwood (already pictured) and Tim Rice – here they are …

With Sir Tim Rice 2014

With Brian Bennett (The Shadows) 2017

MIDEM

Marche International du Disque et de l'Edition Musicale

Possibly the music world's most important festival ever since 1967 – very different from events such as Glastonbury, Reading etc. in that it is largely a business event attended by music executives but also embraces live music along the way.

MIDEM was the brainchild of French film producer, Bernard Chevry who first invented the TV event, MIPTV in 1963 located in the French city of Lyon before moving it to Cannes in 1965.

His idea was to give the music industry a lift early in the new year whereby executives from all over the world could come to sunny (if chilly) Cannes to wheel and deal in a beautiful location.

I first attended the event in January 1971 – my then boss Richard Armitage had registered the company, Noel Gay, after being pressurised by our French sub-publisher, Claude Pascal but he had no idea of what it involved. Neither did I, but he elected me and colleague Andy Petre from the agency division to attend, sending us off in the company Ford Cortina with £100 each in travellers cheques! Quite an adventure, made all the more exciting by the fact the car was not exactly in perfect condition and a broken windscreen on the way to Dover delayed our departure on the cross channel ferry. This resulted in our attempting to drive through the night in order to arrive in Cannes by the following day – the start date of the festival. I wanted to call a halt and book into a hotel but Andy was convinced he could drive us through only to give it up at around 2 am in the centre of a tiny French village in the middle of nowhere. The French Auto Route system was only just being built so our journey involved many national roads (same as the UK's 'A' roads) and even some minor tracks through these little villages. Amazingly we saw a light from a corner bar so ventured in, had a drink and enquired about a room. They had one and we spent an uncomfortable night in a bug-ridden, double-bed with the tap dripping in the form of a Japanese war torcher.

Anyway, we finally arrived in Cannes mid-afternoon the following day and proceeded to register and set up our company stand. It was absolute chaos and proved to me my first lesson on how 'relaxed' the French could be when it comes to organisation. In fairness this was the first festival to be housed in the new Palais des Festival as the, much smaller previous events had been located in the Martinez Hotel on La Croisette. After finally being hooked up for electric power we had the sound system working and we decorated the walls with album covers and posters – we were hugely under equipped!

Once we clicked into gear it became rather enjoyable and the demos we played to various record labels from around the world were being accepted as singles – we then realised how the world respected anything coming out of the UK!

We also realised a massive amount of stamina is required as the social activities would run all night but we had to be back on the stand by 9.30 am every morning, every day for an entire week.

The best thing coming from this, my inaugural MIDEM, was meeting my lifelong friend, Eddie O'Loughlin who was working for New York based record company, Neil Bogart's Buddha Records! Eddie was distressed! I was his shoulder to cry on as he described how he was blitzed by aggressive men demanding their royalties – by the penultimate day he had had enough so he said he would close the stand – I was exhausted, so I also closed and hung out with Eddie. Buddha was a typical New York indie label of the seventies, achieving good success but not always efficient on financial matters. Their roster included The Lemon Pipers, The Tokens, Edwin Hawkins Singers, Melanie, Lou Christie, plus Gladys Knight who came from the Motown label and achieved legendary status with the all-time classic, *Midnight Train To Georgia*!

Eddie moved on to become one of the most successful record man of all time! He worked in A & R for Bob Reno's Midsong International achieving countless hits with Carol Douglas, John Travolta, Silver Convention, Sybil etc. He founded his own label. Next Plateaux in 1980 enjoying even more success with Salt-n-Pepa, Paperboy, Sweet Sensation, etc. After a spell in A & R at Tommy Boy Records and music consultant for The Voice of America TV show, he relaunched the label with yet more success coming from Nina Sky, JTX etc etc. and currently has a senior A & R role with Monty Lipman's Republic Records enjoying huge worldwide success.

Meanwhile, back at MIDEM, my boss Richard Armitage was so impressed with our results he decided to join in the following year and we rented a larger space to facilitate a staff of five. I thought he may cramp my style but to his credit, he allowed me to conduct my multiple appointments without interference. By then I was learning how the sub-publishing world worked and started to appoint representatives from all over the world – great business, huge fun and lovely people.

Thereafter came a consecutive run of visits continuing to this day, although for the first time, the event was cancelled due to Coronavirus in 2020.

Most memorable of these were:

In 1979 when I launched my own RMO Music putting my reputation on the line but overjoyed about the reaction, raising over £200,000 in advances for my new music catalogue.

Next big year was in 1988 at the start of the Sharp End / PWL era. We had all the promotion in place for Kylie's *I Should Be So Lucky* and it was now crucial for the single to chart somewhere in the UK Top 40 as we knew the all-powerful 'Top of the Pops' TV show would follow and would carry it all the way.

The night before the new chart was announced, the team met at the Martinez Hotel bar (until the early hours) – this included Pete Waterman, PWL execs David Howells and Tilly Rutherford, Impulse Strike Force MD, Steve Jenkins, Pinnacle Distribution head, Steve Mason along with me and Robert. At a time when there was no technology to assist, we arranged to telephone our head of press, Sue Foster, back at home in London – this was set for 5 pm when the Radio 1 chart run down started at a phone booth in the Majestic Hotel which was a quieter, calmer choice of venue.

I was armed with a ton of Franc coins (French currency, pre Euro) to feed into the slot. The team were all lined up behind me as we stood in high expectation of the predicted No 38 chart entry. But nothing, nor was it 37; 36; 35; 34 – people started to drift away and soon after it was just me, Robert and Eddie O'Loughlin, who was wrapped up in the excitement of it all, remaining. Finally, it came on the radio at No 31 – we were on our way. Good news travels fast and by the time we finished the call and entered the bar area, Pete Waterman already had the champagne uncorked, the seats all taken so no space for us but this did not prevent some major celebrations later. Moving on to 2001 – Sharp End were appointed by his UK publishers, Peer Music to handle PR for American record producer, David Foster surrounding his 'person of the year' MIDEM award.

A true labour of love – this involved arranging a film crew from MTV to attend and film a behind the scenes feature, plus various radio interviews. Also we were to organise the media at the special presentation dinner at the opulent Carlton Hotel restaurant; attend Peer Music's celebration lunch at the wonderful La Colombe d'Or hotel/restaurant near Nice, where he conducted the radio interviews.

What could possibly go wrong? Well, as I strolled along La Croisette towards the Carlton Hotel on the morning of the filming, to meet David and the MTV crew, I had a call from Warner Records International manger, Mary Hooten informing me that the star turn known as The Corrs (David Foster's major discovery) had cried off sick! So, the centrepiece of the MTV film would not be available, they were also due to perform at the big dinner – what could we do? The TV guys were not bothered, just happy to be in Cannes as the sun was shining.

David then introduced us to a very young, unknown Josh Groban – "He'll do," said the TV producer.

Josh had a very quick briefing from David on how to conduct an interview and he was brilliant. He also was super brilliant at the dinner where he performed three songs in front of the world's most powerful music executives. Josh went on to become the biggest selling artist in the USA in 2007.

Socially MIDEM is right up there – the early live concerts included Stevie Wonder, Elton John, Leo Sayer etc., all magnificently staged at the old Palais des Festival (the new high tech building opened in 1982) followed by several hours drinking in the Martinez bar.

Over the years there have been many memorable lunches and dinners too – for five or six years a group including me, David Mindel and Eddie O'Loughlin enjoyed dinner with various of our other music friends; later my radio friend Phil Swern hosted regular dinners at Auberge Provencale in the old town, also the location for some wonderful Shapiro Bernstein dinners with their top execs Michael Brettler and Debbie Rose. Then we have enjoyed celebrating our friend, American music publisher, Patrick Conseil's birthday at La Colombe d'Or. For many years one of Sharp End's best clients, Eagle Rock Entertainment hosted a drinks party – on one occasion there was an additional invitation to see Justin Hayward perform.

These are just a few examples of events over many years of MIDEM fun and there has never been a disappointing year for me. I first met lifelong friends in Cannes and it has always been a fantastic opportunity to hang out with them and establish new contacts from all over the world. One of my best friends from the seventies David Mindel, who now lives in France organises the 'survivors' lunch every year at the L'Ondine beach restaurant which never fails to delight and we make a point of bringing in new people every year to keep the average age below 60!

Eddie O'Loughlin at the Martinez Hotel, Cannes

Eagle Rock Entertainment's annual Midem party invitation

David Mindel (host)/Judd Lander (plugger)/John Boughtwood (Music Sales Music Publishing)/Peter Knight (Catalyst Music Publishing)/Ron McCreight/David Stark (Songlink Magazine)/Mandy Oates (Eaton Music). Seated is Ray Williams, Elton John's first manager.

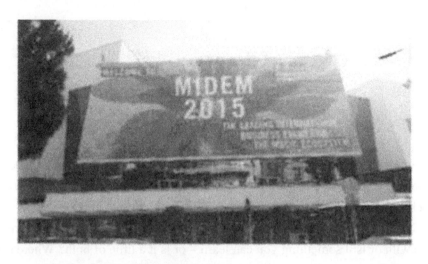

My long time business partner, Robert Lemon with Eddie O'Loughlin at a
'Survivors lunch' January 2010

Chapter 34
The Songwriters

Although for most of my career I have been a record plugger, I also have had strong roots in music publishing – representing songwriters, composers, lyricists and had the privilege of working with some of the greatest in the business.

The art of song writing is hard to define – is it a gift, something you are just born with or is it something you can learn – or is it a little of both? Whereas the Beatles could not read or write music, Paul McCartney is the most successful British song writer of all time! On the other hand, Burt Bacharach was classically trained and learned 'composition' under Darius Milhaud and completed his education at the Music Academy in California. Later he was heavily influenced by jazz – in some ways similar to the UK's John Barry who also discovered jazz and the trumpet while in military service following a classical education from York Minster organist, Francis Jackson. John Barry also studied the Schillinger method as a correspondence course – music by numbers, but there is no doubting his creative ability (countless wonderful movie scores starting with Adam Faith's *Beat Girl*, then all the early Bond movies and way beyond).

The UK's Song writing Academy's Martin Sutton would support the idea that writing/composing is something one can learn (and runs such courses) as would the late Ralph Murphy (Murphy's Law Of Song writing, publ. 2020) who lectured as representative for the American copyright society, ASCAP. Both have had successful song writing careers so they must know something about the art.

Here are some of the truly gifted writers I have worked with either as their publisher or as their plugger – all of them fascinating characters, mostly quite humble considering their massive successes over a long period.

USA

These from New York's Famous Brill Building and 1650 Broadway where promising songwriters clocked in to their 'song writing booths' on a nine to five basis – and then some.

BURT BACHARACH

It was just another day at the BBC but one I will never forget – I was with the truly iconic songwriter, Burt Bacharach for promotion on his 'The Look Of Love – the Burt Bacharach Collection' released by Warner Strategic Marketing in May 2001.

My first and lasting impression, what a perfect gentleman – softly spoken, thoughtful but so interesting and decisive. Burt is arguably the most successful songwriter in history but in all his interviews he relayed his stories with all due modesty although, being based on 50 years of success in Radio, TV, Record, Stage and Film, the sheer enormity of his achievements was apparent. However, Burt was also a perfectionist and once 'lost it' with Adele when she forgot the lyrics during a rehearsal for the BBC's 'Electric Proms' – the then rising star quickly resolved this and performed faultlessly on the show.

Although he enjoyed a three year run on Broadway with the 'Promises, Promises' musical (providing Dionne Warwick with yet another massive hit in *I'll Never Fall In Love Again*), Burt never repeated the stage experience – he found the impermanence got to him with, "Everything shifting from night to night – with a film, once it's right, its embedded forever … if you've got a great take on a record, it's there!"

His perfectionism was probably best demonstrated by the 28 takes at Abbey Road Studios in 1965 when recording Cilla Black's *Alfie* – Burt conducting the orchestra with George Martin in the control room.

Meanwhile on to 2001 and after a full day of radio work, he thanked me sincerely for all MY work, wow – all his interviews were in ONE take!

Burt's early hits included classics such as *What The World Needs Now Is Love* (Jackie de Shannon), *Raindrops Keep Falling On My Head* (BJ Thomas, from the Butch Cassidy movie), *Close To You*, (The Carpenters), *Magic Moments* (Perry Como) but my personal favourite by a mile was *(There Is) Always Something There To Remind Me* a No 1 single for Mod Icon, Sandie Shaw in 1964 – originally recorded by Lou Johnson and Dionne Warwick in the USA.

Sandie's version was a smash in many countries but in America it peaked at No 52 – they never really did get the MOD thing over there. Burt wrote all these great songs but most until the seventies were considered 'commercial pop' (almost could be seen to be a crime to be so commercial, selling out?

However, in the early '80s he parted with writing partner, lyricist, Hal David ending a relationship that had endured for 25 years! However, the ever anomalous Mr Bacharach found a replacement in new wife, Carol Bayer Sager which resulted in hits for Christopher Cross (*Arthur's Theme*), Michael McDonald/Patti Labelle (*On My Own*), Neil Diamond (*Heartlight*) and another for Dionne Warwick (*That's What Friends Are For*).

So after nearly 40 years on the pop charts, what made him so 'hip' in the '90s? Probably his cameo role in the Austin Powers movie, 'International Man Of Mystery' helped, this was considered very cool at its time of release in 1997 but with a good part of his work crossing over to the soul scene he nearly always possessed natural credibility – witness Dionne Warwick (*Walk On By* etc) and Roberta Flack (*Making Love*), but these days reflecting on his success over 70 decades, did this really matter?

I was reunited with Burt in 2005 for promotion on his 'At This Time' album as part of my consultancy with his (then) UK publishers P & P Songs. Again he coolly and calmly worked through a number of radio interviews but always with fascinating content, and again he thanked me very much for my great work – it was nothing Burt!

Indeed, up until the world locked down due to the Coronavirus, Burt was still playing concerts around the world and there will be more business as usual given time!

Lieber and Stoller

In the wake of all our 'pop' successes in 1995, Sharp End took on a long term consultancy with top independent US publishing company, Rondor Music who represented some of the world's top songwriters including Lieber and Stoller whose credits include *Stand By Me*, *Hound Dog*, *Jailhouse Rock*, *Kansas City*, *On Broadway*, *Pearls A Singer* etc. The focal point of our campaign was the Ivor Novello awards in 2000 when they picked up the International Award. During a seven day run up to the event we booked them on to several radio shows (mainly Mike as sadly Jerry was not fully fit), including Radio 1's 'Newsbeat': The incredibly naive presenter asked how they first became involved with Elvis Presley, so Mike disclosed an amazing story about their song, *Hound Dog*: after some chart success with Big Mama Thornton's original version which they also producer, Jerry decided to spend his royalties on a 'trip of a lifetime'. He set sail to Europe on the Andrea Doria ship visiting London, Paris and Rome over a period of several months (no regular air travel in those days). On the return trip the ship was approaching the coast of Nantucket, bound for New York on July 25, 1956, it collided with another liner and 46 people died. When the news reached Mike headed immediately to the site and much to his relief discovered that his friend had survived. At a holding residence nearby, they became reunited and Mike gushed, "Thank God you are still alive" – "I also have some good news: *Hound Dog* is the No 1 single right now." Jerry responded along the lines of that could not be possible as the record peaked at No 12 months back.

"No, a kid called Elvis Presley has covered it so now we have a real smash!"

This stunning story seemed lost on the Newsbeat presenter – she simply said, – "Do you have any more stories like that?"

NEIL SEDAKA

In 1992 Sharp End ran the campaign for a 'Very Best Of Neil Sedaka' for Universal Music and he made himself available for several radio and TV appearances.

The most memorable was his starring role for ITV's Des O'Connor Tonight high rating show, which also featured wacky comedian, Freddy Starr I Neil was accompanied to Thames TV studios in Teddington, Middlesex, by his wife Leba who proved to be highly protective and difficult while Neil was wonderful – *perhaps a case of good cop, bad cop?* During rehearsal, producer, Brian Penders suggested that Neil increase his contribution from two to three songs which meant an even better plug for the album.

However, Leba refused unless Neil was paid a larger fee! The debate continued – Brian Penders was not happy so I just told him to refuse the extra payment as I believed Neil would want to perform the extra song anyway. It was rather annoying that with Leba's persistence, Brian conceded so more money was coming their way.

Prior to dress rehearsal I was consulted over which million-dollar suit Neil should wear for the show – blue, grey, a darker blue, a lighter grey… on and on…

Once dressed, Leba stood guard over Neil. Show time required artists to then sit and wait in the large make up room in the wings of the stage. Again with Leba making sure nothing went array, the makeup girls gave Neil his finishing touches. Then the crazy world of Freddy Starr passes by to say hello to Neil only to grab his protective napkin, spit and blow his nose violently into it before replacing on to Neil's neck – the look on Leba's face was priceless!

The show then went ahead without further incident and as always, Des gave the album a massive plug – again as always, we retreated to the studio bar to celebrate a most enjoyable and successful evening.

With Des O'Connor at a friend's movie themed fancy dress 40th birthday party – he is supposed to be Ewan McGregor, I'm Steve McQueen!

Gene Pitney

Another lucrative deal for Sharp End in 2001 was promoting much of the back catalogue owned by major independent record company, Sanctuary. First release was a 'Best Of Gene Pitney' album and with such a fantastic track record it would not be difficult to set up a string of major radio and TV shows.

I met Gene on the morning of September 11, 2001 and we set off for the first of many interviews planned for that day-this being for IRN (independent radio news) who were based at the nerve centre of news the ITN building, 200 Grays Inn Road, west central London (also housing Reuters and various international news services).

After waiting in reception for several minutes I politely enquired about the delay which fell on deaf ears. After a further period of waiting I pushed further explaining that we had a very full schedule for the day – eventually the production assistant invited us down to the basement 'atrium' where we could see the amazing pictures on the big screens that surrounded us – this was the second strike of 9/11 breaking out!

Gene immediately called home as his son often commuted in to Manhattan from the family home in Connecticut — all was well as he had not travelled in to town that day.

He was then ready to do the interview which did happen but only after a long delay.

Otherwise, everything went to schedule and indeed it gained momentum as Gene rapidly became the celebrity voice of NY on 9/11 throughout the national media. GMTV had previously passed on our offer of an appearance – now they called begging for him to do the show. He was also on the daily National ITV news programmes on three occasions.

During that first day I received a call from the record company – Roger Seaman who was a director of Sanctuary thought we should cancel Gene's welcoming dinner at Mayfair's, Langan's Restaurant as he would be too upset by the events back home. I put this to Gene who simply said – "Well, I have to eat don't I?"

Although Gene initially appeared to be a serious chap, he had a wonderful sense of humour – a few anecdotes:

During a TV interview with legendary presenter, Gloria Hunniford he was asked about the riches he had made from music and what that might get you (in a friendly way, she was trying to be controversial, almost attempting to embarrass him). Shamelessly he answered — "It gets you a huge, beautiful house with a big swimming pool and lots of champagne." The joke was on Gloria!

Close to our office in Golden Square, on Beak Street (London's Soho) was a classic Chinese Restaurant that had been there for many years and Gene had eaten there on countless occasions becoming very friendly with the Maître d' who he called Mr Wong. After all that time he discovered that was not his name at all – what to do, just keep using the W(r)ong name!

Gene found it amusing, not to mention a serious fault in the system that, after all the extreme uplift in airport security (see 9/11 story above), he had travelled thousands of miles throughout the world, on various airlines without realising he had a penknife in his carryon luggage!

Throughout the 1960s Gene enjoyed twenty-two Top 40 hits in the UK and 16 in the USA – most of these Top 10; he also wrote some all-time classics for other artists including The Crystals' *He's A Rebel*, Bobby Vee's *Rubber Ball* (also a Top 5 single in the UK for Marty Wilde) and Ricky Nelson's *Hello Mary Lou*! He sadly passed away in 2006 after a heart attack – rather ironic that he always insisted on a gym being available in his hotels when on tour!

Gene lived the good life and had a career many of today's aspiring artists can only dream of! A really happy man with a wonderful family.

Randy Edelman

(L-R) Iain McNay (Chairman Cherry Red Records), Randy, Me, Renata McNay, David Stark Ahead of Randy's show at the Pheasantry in Chelsea in 2011.

Known for his UK hits with *Concrete and Clay* and *Uptown Up-tempo Woman*, Randy was one of a classic breed of American singer-songwriters who were very much in vogue in the seventies. Quite a character, I really liked him and his wife, another successful songwriter, Jackie de Shannon – more of her later.

On behalf of Cherry Red, I promoted his new album 'The Pacific Flow to Abbey Road' and I had considerable success in setting up many radio interviews. As part of the promotion I invited several Radio 2 producers to his live shows but, in their opinion, Randy's voice proved not to be as strong and it was but his infectious personality really got him through these live performances.

Albert Hammond

My company, Sharp End Promotions became radio and TV consultants to major publishing company, Rondor Music in 1995 and one pleasurable duty was to make some noise for their writer (at the time), Albert Hammond. We were buzzing with ideas for him but he was somewhat reluctant – "Slow down, don't burn me!"

It was a different story several years later when he was signed to Peter McCamley's P & P Songs by which time I was working on my own and they gave me a similar consultancy. Albert had been inducted in to the Songwriters Hall Of Fame in New York on June 19, 2008 and he wanted to mark the occasion with some promotion including a Music Week special advertorial. It was also his 40th year in the business although most people remember him for his own 1972 hit, *It Never Rains In Southern California*; *The Air That I Breathe*, The Hollies; or *When I Need You*, Leo Sayer.

Jackie De Shannon

Another gifted songwriter who also had much success as a performer in the '60s, famously appearing on the same bill as The Beatles in 1964 – she named her album 'Breakin' It Up On The Beatles Tour'. The album included two massive songs, *Needles and Pins* and *When You Walk In The Room* (which Jackie also composed) and became UK hits for Merseyside group, The Searchers! I promoted this and a series of her albums for Cherry Red in 2006. Although her biggest single was *What The World Needs Now Is Love* written by Bacharach and David although her own *Put A Little Love In Your Heart* came a close second. An extremely charming and modest lady considering all the success which included writing the iconic *Bette David Eyes*, a worldwide No 1 for Kim Carnes. A rather nice gesture when she hosted a somewhat dignified tea party for her UK team at the Savoy Hotel during her promotion trip in 2006. Her interviews including the Ken Bruce, Radio 2 feature, *Tracks Of My Years*.

The music publishing business in the USA was extremely different from the UK and there are many more interesting stories in Ken Emerson's 'Always Magic In The Air' (Harper Collins, 2005) including much more on Burt Bacharach / Hal David; Neil Sedaka / Howie Greenfield; Jerry Lieber / Mike Stoller.

The Songwriters – UK

For me being thrust in to the hub of the UK's home of songwriters at the tender age of 16, it felt much more intimate and friendly although not without its dramas – here are some of my experiences with some of our greatest talents in the world of Tin Pan Alley (Denmark Street) based in the West End of London – my first office was at No 24.

Roger Greenaway

One of the most successful British writers in the seventies, often co-writing with Roger Cook (*I'd Like To Teach The World To Sing, You've Got Your Troubles, Home Lovin Man, Good Morning Freedom* also with Albert Hammond/Mike Hazelwood) and Tony Macauley (see below). Roger also wrote several of The Drifters hits including *Sittin' In The Back Row Of The Movies* and *You're More Than A Number In My Little Red Book*, both also with Tony. He was always supportive when I was just a kid around Denmark Street, approachable with time for everyone even when he was churning out hit after hit. The only time I had real business with him was when working The Drifters Greatest Hits album for Warner's. I remember he was completely unaware of the campaign but was delighted when I told him – "I need the PRS fees," he said as I handed him a few copies. At this point of his career he was running the UK office for the American copyright unit, ASCAP.

TONY MACAULAY

MUSIC WEEK MAGAZINE Ad taken by Noel Gay Music, my employers.

Tony was managed and published by my first employers, Noel Gay. Although I was MD of the publishing company at the time of much of his success, I always felt that he was more at home dealing with the Chairman/Owner, Richard Armitage. It was a question of trying to prove my worth to him so I went plugging with one of his biggest ever hits, David Soul's *Don't Give Up On Us* – a No 1 single. Even this was not enough and Tony set me the challenge of plugging his Laurel and Hardy song, *Another Fine Mess* which became the follow up to their No 2 hit, *Trail Of The Lonesome Pine* – in spite of my best efforts it failed to reach the heights of the previous single. I remember setting up radio interviews for Tony (Laurel and Hardy had long since passed) including one for Thames Valley Radio (210FM) which involved me driving from Kent in the very early morning to pick up Tony from his North London flat and then on to the radio station in Reading. Needless to say the traffic was appalling so we were late so I yet again failed to impress Mr Macaulay!

Justin Hayward

At Radio 2 for the Simon Mayo Show, July 2017

Another dream project coming out of our deal with Eagle Rock/Eagle Vision was a long awaited solo album from the Moody Blues' main man, Justin Hayward.

From the outset it was a true labour of love – at the Midem Music Festival in Cannes, January 2013, Eagle staged a private showcase where Justin performed a few tracks from 'Spirits Of The Western Sky' due for release the following month. Around 50 record company executives from all over the world witnessed some magic that late afternoon but Robert (Lemon) and I were privileged to go on to have dinner with Justin and his manager, Martin Wyatt at the famous Gaston de Gastounette by the Cannes marina.

This was followed by several other campaigns including a live DVD/CD of the latest album plus some Moody Blues classics – *Question*, *Nights In White Satin* and *Forever Autumn*. Always charming, always interesting – he agreed to many radio interviews including the Steve Wright Show, Jools Holland and later (pictured above) Simon Mayo in support of his solo tour in 2017.

Graham Gouldman

With Graham at the famous BBC Maida Vale Studios in West London.

Graham's song writing credits are simply monumental – from 1965 with The Hollies *Look Through Any Window* and *Bus Stop* followed by *No Milk Today* for Herman's Hermits, both Top Ten hits in 1966 and both bands originating from Manchester (close to his birth place of Salford). Continuing the Manchester connection, Graham joined local band, The Mindbenders whose lead singer, Wayne Fontana later recorded Graham's *Pamela Pamela* enjoying yet another Top 5 single. Then came The Yardbirds' (featuring top guitarist, Jeff Beck) *For Your Love* (originally recorded by Graham's band, The Mockingbirds), *Heart Full Of Soul* and *Evil Hearted You*. All this before the record breaking success of lOcc who kicked off unprecedented success from 1974 with *Wall Street Shuffle*, *I'm Not In Love*, *I'm Mandy Fly Me*, *Things We Do For Love*, *Arts For*

Arts Sake, *Rubber Bullets* and *Dreadlock Holiday*, all co-written by Graham with lead singer, Eric Stewart.

There was so much more, including WAX a partnership with Andrew Gold, best known for their 1987 smash, *Bridge To Your Heart*.

Many years later, I came in to promote his solo album *Love and Work* which was launched to a packed house of media executives at the BBC Club, Great Portland Street in central London. Along with some new songs, Graham's performance of previous hits including *No Milk Today*, *Bus Stop* and *Dreadlock Holiday* was just sensational. I had the honour of introducing him on stage completing a night that will stay in my memory always.

With Graham at the BBC Club for his album showcase in 2012. Songlink's David Stark to Graham's right & Radio 2/6 Music producer, Mark Sheldon to his left.

Graham's commitment to his music career is total and he has continued to tour with 10cc – I was lucky enough to attend one of their shows at the Royal Albert Hall, their 40th anniversary show on May 10, 2012, where another original member, Kevin Godley made a special guest appearance. With enthusiasm and energy to space, Graham also tours the world as a solo artist under 'A Heart Full Of Songs' banner but he was devastated when his 2020 run was cut short due to Coronavirus. Happily, he is back on the road soon.

I was overjoyed when Graham came back to me eight years later to promote another new album 'Modesty Forbids' which included on track featuring Ringo Starr on drums (Graham had recently toured in his All Starr Band).

Tony Hatch/Jackie Trent

Tony is another of the UKs most successful songwriters in history and a very interesting character too! I first met him in my time at Noel Gay in the late '60s when Tony was enjoying tremendous success, mainly with Petula Clark (*Downtown*, *Don't Sleep In The Subway*, *I Couldn't Live Without Your Love*) – all co-written with his then wife, Jackie Trent!

Also at that time, Jackie's brother Les and his best friend from Stoke, Dave Ions were working for Tony's publishing company but he thought Dave would be better off working with me at Noel Gay and I am pleased to say he did.

In due course Tony and Jackie parted company but strangely, brother Les continued to work for Tony – Les was a fun guy but was obviously under pressure from Tony to keep his songs active as I had many calls for help over the years when I had some record company influence.

Many years later I was commissioned to work on Petula's 'Ultimate Collection' album release by Sanctuary Records in 2002 and was fortunate enough to spend much time with her at the many radio and TV shows booked to plug the album. Petula has an amazing work ethic and even in her advancing years had the energy and enthusiasm for all the shows, without complaint. Also one of the few artists that I have ever worked with that genuinely seemed interested in me – it's usually all about THEM! A highlight was when she played the famous London Palladium when she signed the above photograph for my mother – Tony Hatch was also in attendance.

Strangely six years later, I finally met Jackie Trent and her new husband, a former policeman, thanks to Cherry Red reissuing her 'The Magic Of Jackie

Trent' album which then led to her commissioning me to work on her new 'Trentquility' album.

There was certainly no love lost between her and Tony – there were many legal issues associated with royalty payments etc. They divorced in 2002; Jackie passed away in March 2015 at her home in Menorca.

Elton John / Bernie Taupin / Gary Osborne

Although I never had the opportunity to work with Elton, we have brushed shoulders on occasion. His first music publisher, Dick James (who also published The Beatles) had an office just around the corner from mine in Denmark Street and I was friendly with many of the staff there. One of these, Martin Humphries once came to my office with some demos of a new writer he thought was being ignored and thought I might be interested. One of these songs was *Your Song* – I just told Martin that this was so good that Dick James would never let the song go, nor Elton come to that, it was just a matter of time before he would get the attention he deserved! After massive success in the seventies there was litigation in 1985 as Elton thought Dick had been fraudulent in his royalty distribution – it's part of the old adage that "where there is a hit, there is a writ" – in this case there were several hits and one huge Writ. Elton was awarded a considerable amount in unpaid royalties and the stress of the court case, according to Dick's son Stephen badly affected the publisher's health!

I had worked on occasion with aspiring lyricist, Gary Osborne who wrote and produced an album with Paul Vigrass, managed by employers, Noel Gay. Gary went on to write Elton's lyrics when he temporarily parted with Bernie

Taupin. Those songs included the truly wonderful *Blue Eyes*, *Song For Guy* and *Part Time Love*!

My job writing for US music magazine, Record World included the compilation of a 150 advertorial edition recognising Elton's massive success in the USA – here is an extract of my interview with Dick James in January 1976:

"I met Elton via a number of people who were writing a variety of material – I can't remember all the names but there were couple of the guys from The Hollies who with Elton were trying to write songs together and we put them into an associated company at that time and there were a couple of others who were collaborating with Elton. Although we were doing demos and odd things with them, unfortunately nothing came to light at that time. The whole thing laid an egg. I'm going back to 1965, maybe 1966. Then around 1967 Elton came in and said he would like to work with me and he was looking for a collaborator to write lyrics and did I have any ideas? At the time there weren't many good lyric writers lying around doing nothing. He came in a few weeks or a few months later and he said he was waking up with their boy Bernie Taupin who he had met through some sort of advert."

In fact, it was my friend, Ray Williams, Elton's first manager who took out the advert in the New Musical Express – it was actually asking for new songwriters but it resulted in Elton and Bernie answering the same ad thus bringing them together. Ray was working for Liberty Records at the time but became full time manager before Dick James decided, under considerable persuasion, that John Reid should take over.

Dick James takes up the story:

"It was about this time that my son Stephen had the ambition to set up our own label, feeling that a lot of things he was doing were going into our colleague Larry Page's hands. So on or about January 1, 1968, we set up This Record Company, a production unit; we didn't have the DJM label but we started to produce Elton John and the records went out under a deal that Stephen developed with Philips Records' Fontana label. Then we set up the DJM label with our first artist being Elton. Of course we weren't immediately successful and we suffered quite a little for a while. However, we were getting a modicum of success via the BBC, what one would term a turntable for him but we just couldn't sell the records. Then in 1970, we had the opportunity of selling Elton to the States; by then we'd got Russ Regan (who was then in charge of the UNI label at MCA), interested and he signed Elton to the original licensing agreement between us.

Then we sent Elton to the USA in 1970. We sent him to The Troubadour gambling with a total budget of around $10,000 which at that time was a lot of money. He played The Troubadour in San Francisco and in LA – the second show was POW – that was it, it started happening from there and everything boomeranged back into the UK!"

The 2019 Elton Biopic, "Rocket Man" tells the story but not always entirely accurately, for example my friend Ray Williams has very blonde hair – the actor Charlie Rowe has very black hair!

Ray Williams/Ron/David Mindel   Actor Charlie Rowe with Ray Williams,
At our traditional "survivors"   the real Elton John manager
Midem beach lunch

David Bowie

Someone I would love to have worked with — I missed my chance after hanging out with him at La Giaconda coffee bar in Denmark Street in the early '60s. David was just looking for a break like the rest of us – he didn't have to wait long, and how successful was he…!

The Equals

These guys were school friends from Hornsey, London although Eddie Grant was born in Guyana whilst Derv and Lincoln Gordon's roots were Jamaican. I met them in the most popular Denmark Street watering hall, The White Lion and one liquid lunch seemed to involve me buying all the drinks. After a while I politely enquired if the royalties were coming in, after all they were No 1 with *Baby Come Back* which was also climbing the US charts. Sheepishly they explained they were on Eddie Kassner's President label so the money was not that forthcoming. A few pints later, guitarist Pat Lloyd volunteered crossing the road to the offices, No 25 Denmark Street, right next door to me, to demand some royalties. We had rather a long wait, but Pat eventually returned with some cash – however he was unsure of what he had been forced to sign in order to get it. A lovely bunch of guys and they became regulars in the pub along with Gordon Waller (Peter and Gordon), Johnny Rotton and earlier, songwriters Tony Hiller, Barry Mason, Bill Martin plus others along with most of the music publishing community.

Bill Martin/Phil Coulter

Best known for two massive songs – *Congratulations* and *Puppet On A String* which were both Eurovision Song Contest entries for Cliff Richard and Sandie Shaw respectively. *Congratulations* finished a close second in 1968 but became a No 1 hit for Cliff and an evergreen copyright, used when anyone, anywhere won anything! *Puppet On A String* actually won the contest the previous year and was also No 1 but widely criticised for being too 'cheesy' by Sandie herself along with most music reviewers. Later they wrote and produced a long string of hits for Kenny on Mickie Most's RAK label and other more short-lived artists including Slik and Arrows. In a time when they had something of a magic formula yet more success came with The Bay City Rollers, Richard Harris, Cilla Black and Elvis Presley.

Bill was a real character and in my development years in Denmark Street he would include me when holding court in the local pubs which I hugely appreciated. He actually had his first break with Tommy Quickly recording his song, *Kiss Me Now* in 1963, the year I started work in Tin Pan Alley. However, many years later I was on my long awaited holiday (in Portugal), exhausted after all the Kylie Minogue work, when Bill approached me poolside observing my Kylie T Shirt, demanding a piece of this merch and my presence at the local bar. I then remembered that he had retired to Vale Do Lobo to play Golf but was bored and was desperate for some music business company – I had inadvertently chosen this as my holiday destination. I spent the entire week trying to avoid him! In his crazy youth (and after a few wee drams) he famously pushed the head of Radio Luxembourg into a swimming pool, tuxedo and all after an awards ceremony in the Grand Duchy! I witnessed the occasion and noticed that the radio head in question, Alan Keen was not at all amused and I'm not sure if he ever forgave him. Bill sadly passed away in 2020.

Les Reed/Barry Mason

Lovely couple of guys – Les has sadly recently passed away but he left an impressive body of work which will live on forever. *The Last Waltz* and *Delilah* became standards after becoming breakthrough songs for Engelburt Humperdinck and Tom Jones respectively. As a young fan I admired Les as a member of the John Barry Seven but it was Barry (Mason) I came to know well on the Tin Pan Alley circuit. Barry had a great sense of humour and would always encourage me in my early plugging days. Les also co-wrote songs with several others including another friend, Roger Greenaway, and Geoff Stephens who sadly I have never met.

Stock, Aitken and Waterman

At the PWL Studios, south east London 1988

There can be no doubt these guys were the golden ticket for a hit record for nearly 10 years – they were simply untouchable!

I came in during 1987 at the beginning of PWL Records which was designed to provide another outlet for their songs and productions and this came with the formation of my company, Sharp End Promotions (Pete Waterman being a director) – the full story I have already described.

For Mike, Matt and Pete it started in 1984 with Devine's Top 20 hit, *You Think You Are A Man* which they produced at the Marquee Studios where future colleague, Phil Harding was an engineer. It was a year later when they launched the career of the Queen of High NRG, Hazell Dean with *Whatever I Do* and a further 10 months until the No 1 smash for Dead or Alive, *You Spin Me Round*. This success gave them the platform to open the famous PWL studios in The Borough, near London Bridge in South East London. Still stretched financially, the vastly experience record man who had previously held major positions at CBS and MCA Records, David Howells gave them a helping hand and the business guidance for the new venture – Phil Harding being appointed studio manger.

In 1986 they joined forced with girl band Bananarama and produced a cover of *Venus* which became a No 1 single in the USA and put them firmly on the map – hits from Princess (*Say I'm Your Number One*, Mel and Kim (*Showing Out, FLM* and *Respectable*) followed, proving that the guys had the magic touch when it came to writing songs.

Things really kicked in with Rick Astley's *Never Gonna Give You Up*, arguably the most perfect pop record ever made! This was the track that Pete played to Robert and me to sell us on the idea of going into partnership with Sharp End – it was a no brainer!

The hits just flowed and flowed – next came Kylie, Jason, more from Hazell Dean, Sonia, Big Fun, Sybil, Sinitta, Donna Summer, Cliff Richard, Brother Beyond etc.

I had known Pete for many years before this – we had a mutual friend in Tilly Rutherford who was also a club DJ from Coventry. Pete also had a column in Record Business Weekly so he would often call in to my office in Denmark Street to pick up the latest singles to review. At one time he worked as a freelance club plugger and was employed by Polydor to work on John Travolta's *Sandy*. I was handling the radio and I remember meetings at the record company offices – they were considering putting out a different track from the 'Grease' musical but he told them in no uncertain terms what they should do! An early sign that Pete had great 'ears' – he was probably the best A & R man the UK has ever seen. He was really the ideas man while Matt and Mike constructed the songs and spent the hours in the studio. It is often overlooked how difficult it is to write the perfect pop song and the contribution that the guys made in terms of musicianship. Together they really made history!

In 1990, there had been so many hits that it made sense to release another 'Best Of SAW' album and part of the promotion campaign involved an interview with the three guys on the highly rated 'Des O'Connor Tonight' TV show.

It was a fun day, more relaxed than usual as we did not have to deal with the usual performance aspect of the show. Des was always very hospitable and much of the day involved lunch, afternoon tea and pre-show bar but always discussing how the interview would take shape – I remember saying to Matt how quickly it would pass so to make sure he was ready with fast answers to Des' very easy questions, just designed to plug the album. There had often been an underlying feeling that Pete would always steal the spotlight so, in an attempt to redress the balance, Pete kept quiet – Mike stepped up nicely, Matt kept quiet. Nevertheless, it went well as Des shamelessly plugged the album!

After the show we retired to the bar to discover that Maggie Thatcher had stepped down as Prime Minister and to hear Matt complain that he couldn't get a word in – "It went so fast", aahhhh!

Mike Stock, Matt Aitken and Pete Waterman over looked by Des O'Connor

Phil Thornalley

Phil's golden song I guess is *Torn* (co-written with Scott Cutler and Anne Preven) which never quite made it to No 1 in the UK but was also included in Natalie Imbruglia's 'Left Of The Middle' album which sold an outstanding seven million copies in 1997.

One of the good guys, Phil learned his craft working at Mickie Most's RAK studios in the seventies where many of my friends also started – particularly publisher Jon Crawley and Mickie's brother, Dave Most who was the top plugger of the time and taught me so much.

However, it was only recently that I came to know Phil when I worked on his Astral Drive project, a nod to his hero Todd Rundgren with Phil out front as vocalist and keyboard player. Everything he does has a touch of class and imagination! His first big break came as a producer for the iconic CURE whom he also joined as their bass player. Rather like another great songwriter, Graham Gouldman, bass playing is an added impressive skill – Phil also recently toured playing this part with Bryan Adams!

One of the UK's best, Phil's track record also includes two No 1 singles for Pixie Lott, *Mama Do* and *Boys and Girls* which he also produced. Just for good measure he was also in the studio behind the classic Robbie Nevil hit, *Ca La Vie*!

Jamie Hartman

Another contemporary genius, British writer who has enjoyed amazing success over the past 15 years which kicked off with his own band, Ben's Brother who achieved a Top 20 album with 'Beta Male Fairytales' with the lead single, *Let Me Out* being nominated for an Ivor Novello award! I was lucky enough to plug some of the Ben's Brother albums but in the end it seemed these were a platform for his songs which went on to be successfully cut by many other artists including Will Young (*All Time Love*), making No 3 in the UK charts, followed by hits with *The Wanted*, Joe McElderry, James Bay and more recently the worldwide classic hits *Human* and *Giant* by Rag 'n' Bone Man and the brilliant *Hold Me While You Wait* by Lewis Capaldi. Both *Giant* and *Hold Me While You Wait* were both nominated at the 2020 Ivor Novello Awards for the most performed work, the winner was *Giant*!

Jamie's latest project revolves around the quite unique, Celeste! In just 12 months this 26-year-old singer-songwriter has won the Rising Star BRIT award, the BBC Introducing artist of the year and has appeared on major TV shows including Jools Holland 'Hootenanny', 'The Royal Variety Show' and 'The Late, Late Show' (USA)! After a few years of releasing unsuccessful singles, her signing to Polydor coincided with her teaming up with Jamie and everything changed. They wrote her first hit together, *Stop This Flame* and then the John Lewis Christmas TV commercial for 2020, *A Little Love* with Jamie also taking up the producer's role. Thanks to Jamie's amazing ability, she is now a star, and her first album release, 'Not Your Muse' debuted at No 1 in February 2021!

Jamie's creativity, drive and enthusiasm is quite breath-taking and I have had the pleasure of joining him on many social occasions where again his incredible energy is always evident.

Jamie Hartman accompanying Rag 'n' Bone Man at Laylow pre Brits gig February 2020

Jamie at the BMI Awards 2019

Chapter 35
Music Publishers

Such a vital part of the entire industry but publishers have often been the unsung heroes behind the most essential creatives in the world.

I am fortunate enough to be married to Annette Barrett who is widely considered as the best independent publisher of our time! As I announced in my wedding speech – "I have long since given up working in publishing, but have now married the best one!"

Annette's career started at Carlin Music and she eventually joined State Music where my Gary Benson was signed as an artist. After spells looking after Sting and David Bowie, Annette joined Virgin Music and then Warner Chappell where she was responsible for several major artists including George Michael who became her lifelong friend. During her 10 years with the company Annette became International Director but with major company politics playing their part, she set up her own REVERB 2 in partnership with former agent, Ian Wright. By the time of Ian's untimely death, her company had merged with the main Reverb Music and together a substantial catalogue had been built with Annette being responsible for signing, developing and mentoring several great songwriters/composers including Jamie Hartman, Joe Cang, Matteo Saggese, Peter Gordeno, John Fortis, Ali Thomson and later, Nitin Sawhney. In 2012 Annette's master stroke saw the company merge with North American independent, Reservoir Music thus becoming the major force in the worldwide arena. Annette is also currently president of IMPF.

Annette Barrett (Reverb-Reservoir Music) with composer, Nitin Sawhney who presented her Gold Badge Award at London's Savoy Hotel.

On a less personal level, I have always had huge respect for Nigel Elderton who is Managing Director of Peer Music and more recently became chairman of the Performing Rights Society. I first met Nigel when we were both Tin Pan Alley song pluggers – Peer was then named Southern Music and the fact that he is still with them is great testimony to his unprecedented loyalty. I have enjoyed working with Nigel on various projects over the years including my previously mentioned encounter with David Foster at MIDEM. We also had fun with one of Peer's special copyrights, *You Raise Me Up* which had been recorded by Josh Groban but his record company, Warner failed to recognise it's potential. The lyric writer, Brendan Graham (music was by Secret Garden's Rolf Lovland) was passionate about his song which had previously been recorded by Brian Kennedy and Celtic Woman but quite rightly he thought the Groban version to be the one to make it a "standard".

I helped Nigel and Brendan in their efforts to convince Warners of the song's potential at radio but they were not listening. Eventually boyband Westlife took the song to No 1 in the UK and it became a worldwide hit. However, it was eventually the Josh Groban version that gave the song it's international

205

prominence following a spectacular performance at American Superbowl and has now been recorded by countless artists throughout the world.

Nigel has managed to retain his love of music alongside holding some serious board level positions and he is still one of the nicest guys in the business.

Looking back there are many great publishers who I had the fortune of first meeting on the plugging circuit in my early days. In addition to Nigel, I always had a good relationship with Bob Grace who set up the original Chrysalis Music (he called me for advice) but made his name with Rondor Music, the sister company to A & M Records where yet another originally acquaintance Derek Green presided. Bob went on to run Windswept Music so we worked together in the Sharp End days before he voluntarily left the music business after a long and distinguished career. Another great operator during my formative years was Des McCamley but it was his son, Peter that found music publishing to be his forte and became General Manager at Rondor before joining his MD, Bob Grace at Windswept. After both companies had been sold, I consulted for Peter at his own P & P Songs (the other 'P' was Paul Flynn who is now with Peer Music). Being such a small world, Annette's company, Reverb-Reservoir acquired P & P Songs in 2013. Peter is now Creative Director at another independent, Sentric Music.

When I first set up my own RMO Music, my old friend Peter Knight was first to support me with a sub-publishing deal covering Germany Austria and Switzerland – he was representing Peter Kirsten's Global Music. Later he was there again for Sharp End Music. When Kirsten sold to Chrysalis, Peter was installed as UK manager but also formed his own Catalyst Music which he runs to this day and we enjoy working together on some of his discoveries.

My best friend, songwriter, David Mindel mainly now works with Eddie Levy's Chelsea Music (they are both Blues supporters). I first met Eddie way back during his time with Larry Page's Page One Records (another Gary Benson connection with Larry). I had many a good conversation with Eddie, putting the world to rights during his time with ATV Music but it has been more recently that we have found commercial common ground and I had a particularly enjoyable time when he published David's the UK's Eurovision entry *Still In Love With You* by Electro Velvet in 2015.

There are no excuses from me to highlight all these independent companies as this is where I can most associate rather than with the major corporations who are now sadly lacking in personalities. It has now been 16 years since the wonderfully eccentric, Peter Reichardt headed up EMI Music, where for the best part of his 16 years' service, he hosted a table for lunch every day at The Ivy in London's Covent Garden and his assistant, the lovely Lisa Barker had the chore of finding suitable guests to join him. This could never happen today.

Over the years there have been many small innovative publishers – famously Dick James signed both The Beatles and Elton John, maybe he was just lucky, but he was there! I have already mentioned State Music which was run by an amazing character, Ronnie Beck who believed in QUEEN when no record company would step up for them. Over the years so many of these companies have been swallowed up by either Universal, Sony/ATV Music or Warner Chappell. There is such embarrassment when the honours are given out at such events as the BMI Awards as it is so evident that the company representatives had absolutely nothing to do with the songs in question and were probably not even born when they were written!

With my hero, Steve Winwood and publishers' friend David Stark (Songlink Magazine)
BMI Awards.

Chapter 36
Managers

I have nothing but admiration for all of them! I briefly managed Gary Benson in the seventies, not at all fun for me and I was also in placed this role in the early '80s with Robert (Lemon) when we first left Bronze Records, and we formed R & R Management and Music Publishing. Effectively I had previously been managing Scottish band, H20 while officially their publisher and Robert had a long standing relationship with guitarist, Snowy White who had just released the hit single, *Bird Of Paradise* on indie label, Towerbell. These two artists gave us the platform to build a management company which had been Robert's long standing ambition – I hated the job! Perhaps it was partly due to my main responsibility being to travel to Glasgow, nearly every week to sort out various disputes with six fiery Scotsman that made up H20! We did also manage record producers which was completely different and more enjoyable – Dave Bascombe (Tears For Fears, Mark King) and Tony Cox (Lesley Duncan, The Mechanics, H2O) were both a delight to work with.

It was something of a relief when we 'merged' with Mike Heap to set up Legend Records and publishing so I could revert to my favoured role as a publisher and plugger.

Those who have made a huge success of the job as they had the ability and character to take on the record companies and fight the corner for their artists, include:

Jazz Summers

Possibly the best music manager ever – with Simon Napier-Bell he worked his way through the mire to get WHAM the break they deserved I His * biography published in 2013, two years before his untimely passing tells the story of how he camped out in Sony's New York offices until they agreed to release *Wake Me Up Before You Go* which they had dismissed as a nonstarter. His persistence finally paid off thanks to a junior promo guy taking Jazz's side, convincing some secondary US radio stations to play it – the end result was a US

No 1! The single went on to top the charts all around the world selling over 3 million copies (1 million in the US alone)!

Later, Jazz branched out to form Big Life management and record label in partnership with Tim Parry. I first met Jazz when he looked after Lisa Stansfield who played a star role on the Band Aid 2 single, along with many of the PWL artists. We kept in touch and often met up at 'Top of the Pops' studio when his (then) wife, YAZZ appeared on the show.

Eventually, Sharp End worked on a few of their dance records but more significantly, Nigel Kennedy the extraordinary contemporary violinist who was signed to EMI Jazz was not the most organised of people but he was incredibly driven and it was enlightening to watch him beat up EMI to ensure Nigel had the best possible support. He was also a great team player and he backed our promo efforts through thick and thin. Some of the most successful artists he managed from day one – Snow Patrol, Badly Drawn Boy, The Verve, The Klaxons and (no longer on the roster), London Grammer! The business was a better place with Jazz around.

Big Life, Quartet Books, published 2013

Roy Eldridge

Roy developed his unique understanding of managing artists during his 25 years as A & R Director at Chrysalis Records where he signed a deal with Coventry's based Ska, 2-Tone label and therefore The Specials, Madness, The Beat and Selector joined an already impressive roster! Roy also had the responsibility of recording Hazel O'Connor, Jethro Tull and Billy Idol putting the label right up there alongside others in the indie sector such as Island and A & M! One of the true gentlemen of the business and he would always find time for a chat when I called in their West End offices to see my friend, Roger Watson who was also in the A & R department. Almost into retirement, Roy then joined his son, Sam in UROK management initially looking after Ben Drew aka PLAN B! My clients, Eagle were releasing his DVD which Sharp End were plugging so we looked for some promo time with Ben – such a pleasant opportunity to be reunited with Roy who was very supportive in our efforts. At this time, it was another nice surprise to be placed on their table at the ASCAP awards along with Ben and another unique performer, Paloma Faith! UROK went on to manage Jess Glynne and Tom Odell and are also linked with Liam Gallagher – this is where Roy's professionalism and Sam's energy proves essential.

Andy Stephens

I have crossed paths with Andy throughout my career – I guess we started around the same time but his background was one of recording studios starting with EMI, moving on to Polydor which is where we first met. During the seventies, I invested much time in plugging songs and artists to the major record companies and in some cases an interested A & R man would suggest doing a demo at their own studios (it worked for the Beatles at EMI). On a few occasions, the guys at Polydor put me in their studio where Andy would take the session – always incredibly accommodating and we did our best although nothing ever came of these endeavours. Andy worked his way through the ranks there, often combining with Wayne Bickerton and Tony Waddington, songwriters/ producers and eventually forming State Records where they signed my artist Gary Benson. At Wayne's insistence but without any credit, , Andy and I co-produced Gary's follow up to *Don't Throw It All Away* which he wrote on his own, *You* (he should have stuck to co-writing with David Mindel)! Following a move to CBS (now Sony) Andy was appointed label manager for the EPIC label which boasted George Michael and Shakin' Stevens on their roster. Andy gave us the job of promoting Shaky to appease his manager, Freya Miller – they kept George to themselves! He became very close to George throughout an intense legal dispute with CBS and he eventually left the company to take on George's management. Again I am full of admiration for anyone who could take on this huge responsibility but if that was not enough, Andy went on to handle Susan Boyle – not the easiest job. I am pleased to say Andy is still in touch and we have often started the new year together at David Mindel's legendary 1st January lunch.

Deke Arlon

I first met Deke when his band The Offbeats were represented by Noel Gay and signed to EMI Records who released a few unsuccessful singles, the first being *I'm Just A Boy* produced by the (then) legend, Joe Meek. The band toured relentlessly but it was in acting that Deke found his big break, a long run in the ITV soap, 'Crossroads'! I was still in the accounts department at the time and Deke would occasionally, but discreetly ask me for an advance from the petty cash tin – always repaid I have to add. He returned to his first love, music and was appointed Managing Director of CBS's music publishing division April Music – an incredibly successes time for Deke and the company. Always very driven his destiny was really always in the independent sector and his career blossomed when he set up his own management and publishing company with his wife, Jill. They represented writer/producer, Kenny Young (*Under The Boadwalk, Captain Of Your Ship, Ai No Corrida, Come Back and Shake Me* etc); Chris Neil (Sheena Easton, Celine Dion, Aha, Cher etc etc); actors Denis Waterman and Elaine Paige; presenter Ned Sherrin and many more. I came to work with him in 2002 when he joined the Sanctuary Group where he had responsibility for management and publishing.

I had the pleasurable task of promoting album including compilations by The Kinks, The Small Faces and Gene Pitney. At this time, he also acquired Elton John's Twenty First Artists which brought in James Blunt and the rights to the Billy Elliott musical. After a good run, Deke once again became independent and now looks after the Kinks' Ray Davies and Marti Pellow (*Wet, Wet, Wet*)! An incredible career which has lasted even longer than mine!

Jonathan Dickins

I don't really know Jonathan but he is well known for managing one of the biggest successes of the post millennium period, Adele!

However, I do know his father Barry very well having been in the same class at Gearies secondary modern school. Jonathan's grandfather was Percy, co-founder of the NME, the "go to" music magazine for 50 years (I earlier refer to their massive Poll Winners Concerts of the '60s) – sadly now only available as an online edition. Barry's daughter, Lucy worked for her father's company ITB who represented Adele throughout the period of her world beating success, so it was all in the family until Lucy joined the William Morris agency in 2019. Jonathan's September Management also represents indie art rock band, London Grammer who scored a No 1 album in 2017 with *Truth Is A Beautiful Thing* and were awarded the Ivor Novello award for *Strong* as best song in 2014! The band were originally managed by Jazz Summers' Big Life who, along with partner Tim Parry could always find the best new talent.

Jonathan and father Barry

Louis Walsh

In my experience, sadly Louis had nothing like the standing of above mentioned. His success has been based on sheer bluff – confidence and luck yes, ability and application no!

When Sharp End had grown into the number one pop promoters, we had an 'out of the blue' call from the MD at Polydor Ireland telling us about their new boy band who were destined for No 1 in their native country. He continued, local entrepreneur Louis Walsh had auditioned these young guys who would replace Take That and they had a local hit with their cover of *Working My Way Back To You* (originally by The Spinners) and had recorded The Osmonds' *Love Me For A Reason* but the UK company were not at all interested and would not release the single. He promised to send over the full package of records, videos and merchandise which duly arrived a few days later. Still not sure whether to take this seriously, we asked our press office team, Sue and Liz to show something to the pop mags – they went nuts for it and Smash Hits promised to feature them on their big Christmas poll winners show as "most promising newcomers". Polydor's London office were in disbelief and still refused to release the single but with more and more support building in the media, in the end they had no choice. Louis seemed to develop his own form of stage fright and said he had no time to keep coming to London to accompany the boys so Polydor Ireland asked if we would become their paid UK managers (at Polydor's expense) – no problem for us, we were there with the band anyway. We signed a one-year contract to handle their radio, TV, press and management. When the big day of the Smash Hits Party, 1994 came around, Louis could not resist turning up to soak up some glory but in practical terms, had nothing to bring to the party. As things developed Polydor edged their way in further and further to eventually take over the radio and TV promo, once the job had been done.

Love Me For A Reason peaked at No 2 in the UK with four more Top 5 singles following building to their album, 'Said and Done' launch in August at the Chessington World Of Adventures, Surrey. One of the biggest events we had been involved with, there was a huge turn out with all the key media attending on a glorious summer evening. However, to spoil our day in the sun, during the event rumours were ripe that Sharp End services would be dispensed with – Ronan Keating saying, "over my dead body!"

Later in the evening I decided to confront Louis but as I approached his table he did a runner – his PA in her embarrassment telling me he had gone to the toilet. He never returned! Being such an opportunist, he used this success to build a career which mainly consisted of managing next Irish boy band. Westlife which brought him alongside Simon Cowell who gave him the role in X Factor playing the 'joker' role on the judge's panel.

Nigel Martin-Smith

A key part of the PWL team was Impulse, a 'strike force' who covered all the record stores making sure they had stock and made the returns to deliver the desired chart positions. Main man, Steve Jenkins then became MD at Jive Records who picked up a cover version of *The Time Warp* (from the Rocky Horror Show) by Damian. The track had failed on two occasions but now one of the PWL producers, Pete Hammond had made an impressive remix and Sharp End were brought in to plug it. Damian was managed by Manchester based, Nigel Martin-Smith who also ran a modelling agency.

I distinctly remember talking to Nigel at the 'Top of the Pops' studio, keen to know how he saw Damian's future – we had become accustomed to not settling for one hit with an artist but pursued a policy of one hit should kick off a long term career. However, Nigel was more enthusiastic to talk about a new boy band he was casting in Manchester, Take That! As is so often the case, Nigel found nothing but disinterest from all the record companies, we recognised the potential but Pete Waterman was also not interested although strangely invited them onto his 'Hitman and Her' TV show.

Nigel had no choice other than to record and release them himself so employed Sharp End to take it to radio and TV. Radio 1 were not keen but we did get them on one of their summer Roadshows which had massive impact. In truth the first single, *Do What U Like* was not strong, the follow up, *Promises* was a little better and charted at No 38 so at least we had broken into the Top 40. However, by then, Nigel had incurred huge debts to get to this point and something of a life saver, RCA stepped in with a singles deal having been impressed enough with the progress made. It was still 'touch and go' with the first RCA single, *Once You've Tasted Love* only reaching No 47 but Nigel was unshakable in his belief in the band and convinced RCA to stick with it – then came *It Only Takes A Minute* a fine cover of Tavares seventies' hit which made the UK Top 10. There was no stopping them now. However, Sharp End were no longer involved as RCA insisted that their own in house team did the work, part of a non-negotiable deal, the only one on offer, so we gave Nigel our blessing. After a long successful run with the band, they finally parted company with a bitter law suit involving Robbie Williams not helping, although Nigel returned to manage their come back with a TV documentary in 2005 but that was short lived. He still seems to have a strong business acting as agent in many fields of entertainment.

David Enthoven

I don't know what happened to cause the Robbie Williams dispute with Nigel Martin-Smith, but David stepped in to mentor the (then) troubled singer and worked his charm to get him back on track, developing a highly successful solo career which now spans over 23 years. Robbie's first four albums all went 10 x platinum and all reached No 1 in the UK; there have been multiple hit singles including the funeral anthem, *Angels*, also one of the most played tracks on radio during the late '90s! David sadly passed away in 2016 but his partner in IE management, Tim Clark continues the good work although it was David's vision that resulted in such amazing success against all the odds. Earlier in this book I referred to David offering me a job at EG when I was still at Noel Gay – at that time his partner was John Gaydon and both of them worked with me at the company based in London's Tin Pan Alley. We had a great relationship and one of the most memorable moments of my career was attending a small showcase to hear the first album by King Crimson who they managed and signed to their own label, EG who partnered with Island Records. They also developed and signed Roxy Music and later Killing Joke. David along with Jazz Summers were managers who stood strong against EMI when financier Guy Hands' Terra Firma bought the company with Citigroup's loan leading to the company's demise in 2011.

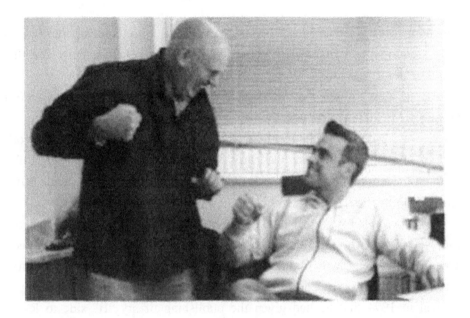

David Enthoven with Robbie

Chapter 37
Pluggers – My Peers

I mentioned earlier that I have outlasted everyone – my contemporaries who were around when I first started either lost their jobs, retired happily, left this world or simply gave up!

My greatest influence at the beginning in 1966 was Dave Most – record producer, Mickie's younger brother.

He was absolutely brilliant although he had some sure fire hit records to work with – at that time Mickie was producing The Animals, Donovan, Lulu, Herman's Hermits, and Jeff Beck before launching his own label, RAK RECORDS in 1969.

I was delighted when Mickie later agreed to produce a Noel Gay managed trio, New World who were signed to EMI but moved to RAK as part of the deal. This meant working with Dave, meaning we would have some fun and almost certainly a hit. However, I do recall that Mickie announced at the MIDEM Music festival in 1971 that he had given the publishing of my "B" side to Radio Luxembourg's publishing company in exchange for a "Power Play". Not easy to confront Mickie but I told him he had no right to do this, not to interfere and I could have secured this slot with giving anything away! The 'A' side was a cover of Lynn Anderson's American hit, *Rose Garden*, a clever 'spot' of a big song by Mickie which went on to give the band their first Top 20 hit.

Dave's biggest successes were probably all the Hot Chocolate and Suzi Quatro hits. After the label's demise, Dave went on to become personal consultant to the BEE GEES before his premature passing in 2010. His humour and enthusiasm were infectious – he really was a one off.

DAVE MOST (third left) with The Bee Gees

In those days much of our work involved hanging out at the various BBC studios (often in the canteens), pubs and drinking clubs where we would compare notes and exchange information. A few of the guys were reluctant to help but Dave and most of the veteran promoters were always very helpful. In particular, I remember Paddy Fleming who worked for CBS (now Sony) who went out of his way to introduce me to some influential radio producers. Paddy's son, Nick came in to the business in 1985 and IS still flourishing – another nice guy and a chip off the old block.

Another special promotion man and influential figure for me was Adrian Williams who I met on the circuit in the mid-seventies when he worked for Don Arden's Jet Records who enjoyed massive success with Jeff Lynne's ELO. A great character, fun but focused – I learned so much from him. As with Dave Most, serendipitously I came to work with Adrian when I formed Sharp End Promotions with Peter Waterman who had signed Rick Astley on a production deal with RCA where Adrian had landed as head of promotion. He carried on this role even once the label had been swallowed up by the Sony giant. What was most admirable about Adrian was his willingness to stand up to radio executives and his superiors at Sony, if he thought he had a strong point – a rare quality when most in his position just play the sycophant but he took no prisoners!

ADRIAN WILLIAMS

He was at the top of his game when he was offered early retirement in 2010 – a good move to accept as working for a major can be a thankless task and having done it all, this offered an opportunity to have a whole new life. I am still in touch with Adrian who loves his new world in Spain but his life could not exactly be described as being 'in retirement'!

Plugging was certainly considered as something of a dark art back in the day and many of the guys considered the best approach was to be slightly edgy, have a gimmick, or arrange a stunt! In the early days we were seen as glorified second hand car salesmen – all that was required was the proverbial 'gift of the gab' with the ability to 'sell sand to the Arabs'!

Another of the great 'characters' from the seventies was CBS (Sony) head of promotion, Judd Lander who is one of the few still active to this day. However, I always consider Judd's laugh a minute style rather old school but he was probably the best ever when it came to gimmicks – magic tricks, bagpipes and even played harmonica on Culture Clubs' *Karma Chameleon*!

Everything changed dramatically as the music business came of age and those on the receiving end of the powers of persuasion becoming wary of the same old pitch and blag!

Those depending on the old school style quickly fell by the wayside. Others were shrewd enough to develop their own way but large amounts of stamina, self-belief and persistence has always been required. As more and more music was featured on radio and TV, a more professional approach was required – it became not just about getting airplay but booking, arranging and organising interviews and live performances for related artists. This was something all of us at Sharp End had great pride in undertaking and never was so much achieved by so few!

I always loved the art but there were many who used the job as a stepping stone to other roles – notably John Reid who became Elton John and Queen's manager; Lucian Grange now Chairman and CEO of Universal Music – he started at CBS's publishing company involving song plugging; Muff Winwood (Steve's brother) gave it a go for Island Records after his period of stardom with the Spencer Davies Group and before he became head of A & R at CBS, later SONY.

I have met some wonderful people throughout the decades – in addition to the above, there were some great characters: Tony Hall, man of multiple talents: DJ, manager as well as plugger handling the careers of Jimi Hendrix, The Who, Dusty Springfield, Scott Walker, Joe Cocker and The Zombies, before doing just about everything for the Real Thing and Loose Ends – he sadly left us in 2019 at the good age of 91 – I wrote this tribute published in Music Week:

'He was one of 'us' from back in the Tin Pan Alley days. He presented the Joe Loss show every Friday from the Playhouse Theatre, introducing all the top bands of the day including The Beatles, The Stones, The Bee Gees, The Small Faces. He plugged some of the best (Hendrix, Joe Cocker) and just had sheer belief in those he rated. Unlike many of the ego-ridden crooks of the time, he was in it for the music and helped anyone of the like. Many years later we shared offices in Golden Square where he continued to manage some wonderful artists to whom he remained *totally dedicated* - The Real Thing, Loose Ends. Overused phrase, but he really was a legend. RIP Tony.' *Ron McCreight, TV and radio promoter*

TONY HALL

Then there was Bill Fowler who handled TV for Warners, Salli Griffin (radio); John Reed (not Elton's man) who also handled TV for RCA and headed up Polydor, a fine example of efficiency; Eric Hall – EMI plugger in the seventies but later found more suitable roles as a football agent and local radio presenter; Richard Perry who was another RCA promo guy, who I first met when Kylie signed for them in 1994, we (Sharp End) were hired as independents and as part of her deal, to do his job (awkward), but he handled the situation with style and grace. He went on to become one of the most successful independents himself – that's what you call good Karma! Also noteworthy are Julian Spear who once headed up the A & M Records promo department but made a good fist of being an indie and Jeff Chegwin (Keith's and DJ Janice Long's brother and sister respectively) who had an inconsistent career until he teamed up with a bright newcomer Mike Grocott who nearly worked for me at one time!

However, such a tough and demanding game produced many casualties – so many could just not last the pace or keep up with an ever-changing landscape, but a few dubious characters still claim to have been a crucial part of major stars' success. I have lost count of how many pluggers claimed to be part of such careers of The Beatles, Michael Jackson, George Michael, Madonna, Britney Spears, Abba, The BEE GEES etc., whereas they just happened to "be in the room" when it all happened. In the end to retain any personal self-esteem you have made a real difference in an artists' career, otherwise, who are we, or they kidding?

A combined package of a great song and a well-managed, talented artist are the keys, as any plugger is only as good as the record he is selling, but as an independent, making those A & R judgements is a crucial part of the job!

Chapter 38
The Finale

I prefer never to say it's the end, rather that it is the beginning of something new and for me, in the twilight of my career I am now reflecting more on the past and a future outside of the music business.

2020 will always be known as the year of the Coronavirus pandemic which changed everything. However the music business had changed beyond all recognition before then, with streaming replacing the traditional way in which people listen to and buy music – record shops have been replaced by the faceless, cold digital world of Spotify, Apple Music, You Tube and Amazon. The heart and soul has been ripped out of the musical arena!

This may appear to be a rather sceptical view of things but I really believe I have had the best of it, especially having the good fortune of being right there at the beginning, in the sixties and beyond. The intense excitement of events such as going to the Wembley Arena (then the Empire Pool) for the NME Pollwinners concerts which starred The Beatles, The Stones, The Who, The Small Faces, Cliff and the Shadows, The Moody Blues, The Yardbirds, the list just goes on and on...; The London Palladium to see the Sunday night TV spectacular headlining the Beatles; The Marquee Club night after night to see most of the above plus Jimi Hendrix, The Spencer Davies Group, The Move, Yes, Long John Baldry, Alexis Korner, etc.

Then there was the feeling of elation, waking on a Saturday morning in anticipation of visiting my local record shop to check out the latest releases and then with some luck and negotiation emerging with a new single and occasionally an album – everything was shiny and new, and somehow quite magical.

Then in 1963 actually to become part of the business and eventually work alongside some of my heroes I had long admired, was simply beyond my wildest dreams. This gave me the opportunity to see and hear more wonderful music, up close at live radio and TV shows – Radio 1 hosted lunchtime performances from the Playhouse Theatre in Northumberland Avenue (central London) where I first discovered the Bee Gees, The Tremeloes, Georgie Fame and many others. TV was all about 'Ready, Steady Go', 'Top of the Pops' and 'The Old Grey Whistle Test' (mainly hosted by my friend Bob Harris). All very different shows – TOTP was a just mental, an adrenalin rush through seeing major artists perform (or for some periods, mime) their current hit and I became a big part of it all especially in the eighties and nineties with the PWL/Stock, Aitken, Waterman releases.

RSG was simply super cool, presented by MOD icon, Cathy McGowan; The OGWT was more of a cultural experience with Bob and his production team introducing us to some of the world's finest, perhaps best described at the time as 'album artists': Alice Cooper, Todd Rundgren, Nils Lofgren, BB King, Bruce Springsteen, The Doors, David Bowie, Bill Withers, Leon Russell, Fleetwood Mac, George Benson, Tom Petty, Muddy Walters, Tears For Fears, Rita Coolidge, The Beach Boys, The Doobie Brothers – for me these were the most memorable performances, but the list is endless. Something of an American bias but at the time the show was the best means of being introduced to artists who were otherwise unreachable. Later I was privileged to work with George Benson and The Doobie Brothers! I suppose the biggest difference these days is that success is harder to measure – the singles chart now seems irrelevant as streaming is driven by repetition – the digital platforms require no effort and very little expense is involved in listening to a song. Until the turn of the millennium music fans only way to 'buy' music was to part with their hard earned money and visit a record store – so much more endeavour involved, but it made the charts much more meaningful. Of course there were a few who liked to 'hype' their single into the Top 40 and occasionally this practice proved successful but in the main the best records rose to the surface and their genuine popularity is in their durability with most of these songs still being played on the radio, synched into film or TV commercial and STREAMED!

It seems that real music fans of today have reverted more to the live music scene which was flourishing at all levels until the pandemic hit in 2020 but will eventually return to its previous heights.

What is encouraging is the level of talent that is still prevailing. Although for me personally those bands emerging in the sixties and seventies were the best, there have been some sensational new names breaking through more recently: John Mayer, Foo Fighters, The Killers, Razorlight, Snow Patrol, Muse and the Manic Street Preachers have all sold millions of albums in the traditional way! In the pop arena writer/producers Jamie Hartman, Mark Ronson and Jamie Scott are exceptionally talented plus Steve Mac (One Direction, Ed Sheeran, Anne-Marie etc) matches the brilliance of Stock, Aitken, and Waterman of the eighties/nineties and significantly Steve has the same manager in David Howells.

However, in the words of Razorlight's Johnny Borrell, "The current crop of chart stars spends too much time on their smart phones promoting themselves rather than honing their skills."

In a national press interview in May 2020, he also took aim at radio stations for focusing on mainstream music, insisting there is still an appetite for rock bands.

Johnny has a point in that the UK's largest national station, Radio 2 has recently adopted a music policy favouring the bland 'mainstream' pop lightweights, rather than championing the more worthy singer-songwriters and bands that boosted their ratings in previous years. It really is unbelievable that such important talents as John Mayer, Norah Jones and indeed Razorlight themselves are rarely heard on the radio. Having said that the BBC's digital music station, 6 Music has filled a large gap and play some quality music but can be a little too 'alternative' to be widely effective (with the exception of the Sleaford Mods who had a No 1 album in May 2020, largely down to spins on 6.

In some ways, this is history repeating itself from the early seventies when Radio 1 ignored the world beating Rolling Stones, Pink Floyd, Jimi Hendrix, The Eagles, Motorhead, Led Zeppelin, The Ramones as well as all the great American soul singers, to favour what they considered to be more popular singles by artists such as Pickettywitch, Vanity Fair, Chicory Tip, The Dooleys, The Osmonds, and The Bay City Rollers – it is all subjective but I believe you could say that such artists did lack credibility and certainly there was no 'soul'! The highly respected DJ, Johnnie Walker famously refused to play anything from the playlist compiled by the Radio 1 committee of the time, preferring better music and went out on a limb with new bands The Sutherland Brothers and Quiver, Stealers Wheel, Humble Pie d Page 161 and most things rock or rhythm and blues based. This resulted in Johnnie being fired but he kept the faith and came back with a bang after a stint on American radio and is still on national radio today. Thankfully Radio 1 always gave the legendary DJ John Peel the freedom to play what he chose on his evening show and he had a great ear for quality as well as 'crossover' artists. A prime example would be Tyrannosaurus Rex who started as a very hip "prog band" and fronted by Marc Bolan became T Rex who enjoyed a string of pop hit singles with irresistible hooks, but there was always quality in Mr Bolan's music!

One of the toughest things about being a plugger is having to suffer the opinions of largely musically unqualified radio programmers! Although we always accept that it is always a matter of opinion, some of their decisions are simply bizarre but they are the people who have the power and responsibility of selecting those tracks and artists to support.

I have always applied the rationale that radio producers are just that – they are RADIO, not MUSIC people, there is a huge difference. The great music men of our time were all visionaries – Clive Davis, Ahmet Ertegun, Berry Gordy, Joe Smith, Alfred Lion, Muff Winwood, Kalder Marshall, Seymour Stein, Eddie O'Loughlin, George Martin, Chris Blackwell, Jerry Moss, Derek Green, Doug Morris and Russ Regan all had credentials way beyond any radio executives, but at some time in their illustrious careers, had to take the rejection of their music by a radio station 'on the chin' – an absurd situation but it has always been the same. In my own modest way, having surrounded myself with music from an early age, played in a band, having the privilege of working closely with so many great artists, sitting in at the best recording studios and attending every kind of gig from the smallest pub to the major arenas and accomplishing consistent success enduring all trends, I think I have a far better idea of what makes a great record than most radio producers. I have often taken comfort from the words of Theodore Roosevelt (US President 1901–09) in his famous speech (extracts): "The credit belongs to the man who is actually in the arena..."; "It is not the critic that counts..."; "There is no effort without error and shortcomings..."; "The man who at the best knows in the end the triumph of high achievement and who at the worst, if he fails at least he fails while daring greatly..."; His place shall never be with those cold and timid souls who know neither victory, nor defeat!"

I have suffered many of such timid souls but feel I eventually came out the winner.

the innovative MUFF WINWOOD from the

Davis Group to record producer (Dire Straits etc.), to world's top A & R man at CBS/Sony.

However, this is the game and although it can be very frustrating, it is also the best fun and the heat of the challenge is irresistible. As long as we have these talented artists, musicians, songwriters and producers, there will always be a demand for music and the means to access it – radio still prevails but for how long… streaming is the thing, but vinyl is making a comeback, time will tell!

A few thousand words ago in my introduction. I described an (un)typical day where I managed to secure a Radio 2 play listing for a new artist – now as I complete my writing, rather neatly history has repeated itself with Sheffield based singer-songwriter, John Reilly's single *La La La (Bulletproof)* getting added at Radio 2 at a time when it has become almost impossible with the station looking for a younger audience and favouring the likes of Dua Lipa, Justin Bieber and Miley Cyrus.

So, we have a very happy ending.

I have been extremely fortunate to work in an industry that largely embraces wonderful characters several of whom have become lifelong friends and there has never been a dull moment so, thank you all for the music!